DECORATE
WITH FLOWERS

This book is dedicated to our dear mothers,
Christine and Akiko, for planting their
love of flowers inside of our hearts
at an early age and inspiring us always.

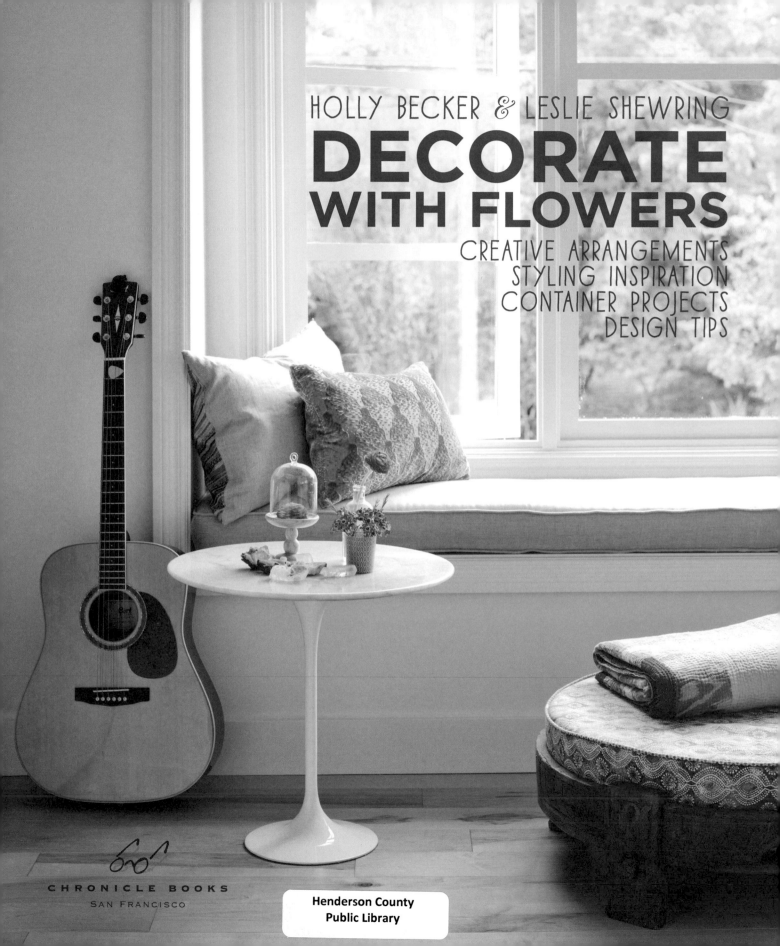

HOLLY BECKER & LESLIE SHEWRING

DECORATE
WITH FLOWERS

CREATIVE ARRANGEMENTS
STYLING INSPIRATION
CONTAINER PROJECTS
DESIGN TIPS

CHRONICLE BOOKS
SAN FRANCISCO

Library of Congress
Cataloging-in-Publication
Data available.

ISBN: 978-1-4521-1831-4

Manufactured in China

Stylists: Leslie Shewring, Holly Becker
Styling Assistants: Jessica Senti,
Diane Shewring

10 9 8 7 6 5 4 3 2 1

Chronicle Books LLC
680 Second Street
San Francisco, California 94107
www.chroniclebooks.com

CONTENTS

INTRODUCTION

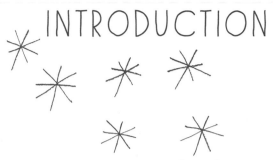

We love flowers, and through our work as stylists, we frequently bring them into our rooms and vignettes to create a little magic. Like most of you, we're not trained floral designers—we simply love to play and experiment, and this book will encourage you to do the same. We are inspired by beautiful flowers, from their colors to shapes, patterns, textures, and scents, and because they are so readily available, you can pull together a fresh bouquet that makes you happy within minutes. Flowers add an incredible lift to any space, and a dinner party isn't complete without them. Most major life events present opportunities to give gorgeous blooms to uplift, encourage, console, thank, show love, or share joy, and they are a popular go-to when we simply want to treat ourselves. They can be deeply sentimental as a result and hold a special place in our heart. Flowers connect us to one another, and to nature, and for all of these reasons it makes sense that we delight in displaying them at home.

We decided to write *Decorate with Flowers* to blend our love for botanicals with our passion for interiors. Our mothers passed on their love of gardening, landscaping, and floral design to us, something we are deeply grateful for. Holly's mom was trained in floral design before Holly was born and continued to arrange for years; she even did the flowers for Holly's wedding, and today she can still whip up an arrangement in seconds that is nothing short of inspiring. Leslie's mother is also a flower lover; as a Japanese Canadian she comes from a culture with a deep understanding and respect for nature. Her mother continues to share her love of gardening and flowers with her children and grandchildren. From a very early age Leslie learned about everything from how to grow and cultivate flowers to their handling and care, and how to beautifully arrange them in a natural way, which is often noted about Japanese design—their genuine passion for purity and a certain flair for stylish simplicity that often comes so intuitively.

There are many gorgeous books which cover how to make professional-looking arrangements that are inspirational and gorgeous. We are not claiming to be a replacement; in fact, we own many of them in our own libraries. But the truth is, neither Leslie nor I take a very serious or overly professional approach to flower arranging. When we are decorating our homes, entertaining, or styling spaces for our clients, we tend to follow our heart and be more spontaneous. Both of us can scan a farmers' market or grocery store and instantly know which bunches will come home with us and where we intend to place them for maximum results. Upon arriving at home, we'll unwrap and clip as we busily put together something driven by our gut instinct. For us, this comes easily, but it's not always so easy for others, which led us to the idea of creating this book. Our goal is to present flowers that are budget-friendly and easy to find and show you how to quickly arrange them, along with lots of decorating tricks and tips. We thought to create eight flower stories, taking you through a variety of home styles to show you how to use flowers in every interior. We've also added a bevy of ideas for choosing (or making) containers, including some step-by-step projects that you can try at home.

It is our heartfelt desire to bring you a fresh approach to decorating with flowers through this book, and to remove the intimidation that is typically associated with floral design. Nothing about our work is traditional or rules-oriented, so if you're on board with that, we guarantee you an inspiring journey. So sit back, relax and see what we have to share.

Happy Decorating with Flowers!
Holly & Leslie

SHEET OF PAPER
OR A BROWN PAPER BAG
TO PROTECT
YOUR PREP SURFACE

FRESH FLOWERS
+ GREENERY

METAL BUCKETS

CELLOPHANE TAPE

JARS AND VASES

FLORAL SCISSORS

VARIETY OF TWINE

WHAT'S IN OUR CABINET?

When you decorate and make arrangements mostly for your own home, you learn over time what your trusty go-to items are, don't you? Our motto: Keep it simple! On the road, we don't have time or space to carry extensive toolkits filled with styling supplies. In fact, we usually pack our favorites and, when we arrive on location, combine them with whatever the homeowner has on hand to aid us in our arrangement making. When working from our individual studios, our cabinets stock only what we use on a regular basis because, as with any hobby, you can easily overstock and end up using only a portion of the gorgeous tools you've invested in. We're certain the pros stock everything from flower frogs to floral adhesive in their shop closets, but like most of you, we aren't in the business of flower arranging, so our approach is affordable and no-fuss in order to obtain a more effortless look.

Always, always, always keep your tools clean, in top shape (scissors sharp!), organized (sort ribbons by color into clear bins), and in a single place so that when you only have 15 minutes of prep time for your guests, you know just where to go to beautifully pull together your bundles of hydrangea, cosmos, and honeysuckle in record time.

HERE'S SOME TRUSTY TOOLS THAT WE TURN TO AGAIN & AGAIN:

★ Brown paper, grocery store paper bags, or newspaper to protect surfaces during prepping

★ Packs of floral preservative packets (the little plastic pouches that usually come with flowers)

★ Metal buckets, always cleaned after use with a few drops of bleach and some water

★ Rags for clean up and for leaf removal on stems with thorns

★ Floral tape for wrapping bouquets—clear or green, it becomes more sticky as you stretch it

★ Flower clippers (we like the Japanese ones with the black handle shown opposite). Floral clippers should be what you invest the most money on.

★ Cellophane tape to create a grid on the top of your container to keep flowers in place

★ Pruning shears for trimming branches. Always trim on an angle and snip into the bottoms making a cross shape so branches can hydrate more quickly

★ Twine, baker's string, and lots of pretty ribbons for securing and decorating

★ Jam jars in all sizes to waterproof containers that can leak, such as tea tins and baskets

★ Assorted vases

★ Rubber bands to bind stems together as needed

★ Wreath frames in green and white

★ Various wires—particularly helpful when creating wreaths on frames

★ A few wire hangers from the closet (see pages 36–37)

★ Corsage pins (optional)

OVERVIEW OF FLOWERS

The joy of flower selection—we love it! There's nothing like scouring for cut flowers at the local florist, grocery store, or farmers' market. You can also forage your favorites from your own balcony garden, backyard, or pick them from your mother's garden. Whether harvested or selected from a store, it's important to know the basics when it comes to choosing, preparing, and working with your blooming beauties. We've outlined a few key points that have helped us over the years, learned mostly through *much* trial and error (ahem!), with hopes that you can take away what makes sense to you. Enjoy!

CHOOSING

It's easy to see a fantastic bundle and exclaim, "You're coming home with me, guys!", but remember that not all flowers are fresh just because they look vibrant in the store. In fact, some can disappoint and be dead within a day. To avoid wasting time and money when choosing flowers, it's key to consider the following:

★ Feel the heads directly under the bloom. Are they firm and plump? With roses, the firmer the head, the fresher they are. If you want flowers that are a bit more open or relaxed, look for blooms that aren't as stiff or tight. When styling interior spaces or working on wedding flowers, you may require ones that are already open or beginning to open up to convey the right look or feeling. Tip: You can open your blooms more quickly by adding them to warm water.

★ If petals are translucent (bruised), have brown spots, are sagging, or the foliage is broken, move on.

★ Look for leaves that are green and vibrant.

★ Some blooms may require a bit of a shake to check whether they are fresh. If blossoms scatter to the floor like snowflakes, this flower is past its prime!

★ If you're picking flowers from a garden, avoid doing so in the hot sun —wait until later in the day or early morning. Flowers are most hydrated in the morning and evening, and tend to dry out during the day when the sun is at its peak. Clipping them at the right time is crucial to how long they will last once collected and arranged.

★ When picking outdoors, beware of insects that bite or sting, since some flowers tend to attract little passengers and you don't want them coming home with you. Also exercise caution around weeds that are growing among flowers, like poison ivy or stinging nettle—ouch! We must add to also use caution when harvesting if you suffer allergies.

★ Be mindful of sap. If buying flowers from a store, they've already been conditioned, but if you're picking from the garden, the sap from certain flowers (like daffodils) can harm other flowers in your arrangement. The best idea in this case is to separate your flowers for the night and then combine them in the morning to avoid any fatal flower combos!

★ When buying flowers for a special dinner you may want to go to the flower shop the day before, as some blooms need a day to open after being in the florist cooler. Create your table arrangements the night before and by the next evening your flowers will have opened beautifully.

PREPPING TECHNIQUES

★ Remove all paper, rubber bands, and ties, leaves that will fall below the water line, and any dead or wilted blooms.

★ Immediately cut the stems on a 45° angle so they can drink in more water, and place them into clean buckets of lukewarm water. The pros suggest cutting under running water so that the stems can absorb it versus air. Leave as much length to your stem as possible since you do not yet know how they'll be arranged; you may need their height depending on the vessel you choose.

★ Clip flowering branches, such as cherry blossom, at a 45° angle then cut into the bottom about ½ inch deep, once, then twice, making an "X" shape to open up the stem so that it will take in more water.

★ Remove all foliage that will sit below the water line since they can collect nasty microbes once submerged—bacteria are never a good thing.

★ If your flowers have thorns, you can remove them with floral snips or a small knife.

★ For a quick way to remove leaves, put on a garden glove and with a slightly damp rag run your hand down the stem in a quick top-to-bottom motion. Done!

'JOHANN STRAUSS'
ROSE

CHIVES

OPIUM POPPY OR PAPAVER

'SARAH BERNHARDT'
PEONY

LIME HYDRANGEA

'CORAL CHARM' PEONY

SPANISH LAVENDER

STACHYS OR LAMB'S EAR

11.

DECORATE
WITH
FLOWERS

BASIC MATERIALS BY CATEGORY

Knowing a little about how to use and work with flowers when arranging goes a long way. Here are some of the categories outlined by pros that you should know:

★ Base Foliage—Sturdy stems that give you a great foundation to work from. Criss-crossing stems in a grid arrangement in the vase can be a terrific way to keep flowers in place. These should be the first materials placed in the arrangement.

★ Focal Flowers—The large, dominant show-stoppers that will act as your focal point. Not all arrangements require focal flowers, but they definitely add a great deal visually. These are generally the next to be added.

★ Secondary Flowers—Slightly smaller than your focal flowers and help to give your arrangement shape and fill in empty spaces.

★ Fillers—Can consist of small flowers, berries, greenery, herbs; anything that takes up space and offers structural support to your focal and secondary flowers.

COLOR, SIZE & SHAPE

★ If you want to mix things up color-wise, but aren't sure where to begin, use your home as your first source of inspiration. It's always a good idea to make sure your flowers fit into your surroundings, rather than clash. Ask yourself, what colors in your room do you want to highlight? Is it the orange and red in your kitchen? Or perhaps you've been longing to mix in a bright hue, like yellow? Put thought into your interiors before hitting the flower shop.

★ If you are scared to go too crazy with color in your arrangement, stick with harmonious shades that naturally work well together, such as red, pink, and purple.

★ Look at your room and think of what color is missing that could be added through flowers. Perhaps your neutral space could use a shot of bold violet? Or your black-and-white living room could really use a shot of yellow?

★ Work with a variety of sizes and shapes. Flowers can have flat heads, dome-shaped heads, a romantic spiral structure, or lots of petals. Flowers with sharp-looking edges like spiky dahlias are very sculptural, as are gladiolas with their sword-shaped stems. Next time you're at the local florist, pay attention to shape and size and work with those you've not tried before.

★ Using a few different sizes of flowers also helps create a beautiful arrangement. Having one or more large round blooms paired with some small spray flowers and a few skinny tall flowers creates texture and interest in your arrangement.

★ Remember, a pop of allium in a vase can be all that's needed to dress up your living room—you don't always need to create an entire arrangement.

STABILIZING YOUR ARRANGEMENTS

★ Flower frogs, which give your flowers a base to sit on in the bottom of your vase, can be handy to keep around though, honestly, we didn't use them in this book. You can find flower frogs in many shapes, materials, and sizes online or in craft stores, garden shops, or ask your local florist.

★ If you have chicken wire, shape it into a loose ball and press it snugly into place at the bottom of your container. This can help hold stems firmly in place.

★ Arrange a bunch in your hand, add a rubber band to hold them together, and add to your vase.

★ Use only opaque vessels for flowers supported by flower frogs or chicken wire, or tied with twine or rubber bands.

★ Create a grid pattern across the top of your container using scotch tape to hold stems in place. You can also use waterproof green floral tape if you are able to conceal it beneath your flowers. We generally create a grid by placing two strips of tape running parallel across the container opening and then three strips running perpendicular across those two.

TIPS FOR FRESHER FLOWERS, LONGER

★ Refresh water daily or at least every few days.

★ Clip stems when you refresh the water. Remove dead leaves and petals.

★ Keep them away from ripening fruit and older flower arrangements since ethylene gas can trigger the aging process.

★ Do not place flowers in direct sunlight, near heaters, or in drafty areas.

★ Keep away from cigarette smoke.

★ Phototropism is when a flower tends to bend towards the light, and some flowers are more prone to this than others. If you place an arrangement on a windowsill you may notice that it begins to curve towards the outside. Sunflowers, buttercups, ranunculus, tulips, and arctic poppies are a few you may have noticed bending towards the strongest light source in your home. Arrangements containing these flowers are best kept away from direct light sources if you want to maintain the style in which you've arranged them!

★ If your flowers came with one of those small packets of preservative, add it to your bucket as it helps to ward off bacteria. If you make lots of arrangements, you can buy floral preservative in bulk. If you have none on hand, add a tiny drop of bleach to the water—it's better than nothing!

To find out how to make this
unusual bottle chandelier
turn to pages 60–61.

13.

DECORATE
WITH
FLOWERS

SAGE

LOVAGE

CHIVE

BASIL

ROSEMARY

PARSLEY

WINTER SAVORY

THYME

MINT

OVERVIEW OF HERBS

Herbs abound! From the culinary variety to those used for tea and medicinal purposes, you can find fresh bunches almost anywhere. With the growing popularity of gardening, more people are growing their own to add to meals and teas. Many prefer to cook with fresh ingredients now more than ever, particularly with the overbearing amount of pre-packaged meals and fast food all around us. Growing herbs on the windowsill in your kitchen can make cooking more rewarding and tasty—there's nothing like using fresh ingredients that you've grown yourself! Farmers' markets have also increased in popularity since many feature local foods grown naturally or organically and give us the chance to consume locally grown food while interacting with a variety of foods that we may not have access to at the grocery store—and they stock a great selection of herbs. And don't worry . . . it is relatively easy to grow your own on a balcony or in a garden if you don't have easy access to them otherwise. But this isn't a cookbook, is it? So why on earth are we talking about herbs?

In addition to cooking with herbs, have you thought to use them as greenery in your floral arrangements? Not many consider this as an option, but they can be terrific as either base foliage or as fillers to add a soft look. Herbs can create a more natural "custom" look when combined with grocery store or florist-bought flowers, too.

It's often difficult to find interesting greenery to add to arrangements—the usual suspects tend to be fern, medium to large leaves, and whatever the flower shop happens to have in stock. Using herbs as your greenery for the dining table or around your home is a simple way to add variety, scent, beauty, and a unique "fresh from the garden" touch to your bouquets. You can also use herbs on their own—no flowers needed. A bowl filled with chamomile or sprigs of lavender placed into glass bottles can be all that's needed to bring life to a kitchen shelf.

HERBS WE LOVE

Mint looks particularly lovely paired with garden roses. In this book you will find many kinds of mint because each tends to have a slightly different leaf. You'll find apple mint, chocolate mint, peppermint, variegated peppermint, and spearmint.

Rosemary paired with mint is also a winning combination —each has a different green texture, bringing dimension to an arrangement.

Sage is another favorite. It looks great in smaller arrangements because its leaves are such a distinct delicate green, and it looks particularly fabulous when combined with white and cream-colored flowers.

Thyme adds a small-scale leaf to a table-top arrangement —a few sprigs tied with twine along with a small spring bloom are so charming when placed in a dainty cup near the kitchen sink or when tied to a dinner napkin.

Chive blossom can be used as a unique accent flower—a look we are quite fond of.

Chamomile has lovely little filler flowers that add a pop of sunny yellow and a sweet, romantic touch.

Lavender is always a favorite for its scent and it makes a great finishing touch to flower arrangements with its distinct color and cone-shaped clusters.

CARE

As with flowers, it is important to clean the stems of herbs before use and to remove all leaves that will sit below water level. Cut the stems at a 45° angle to maximize water intake so that they'll last longer. If you buy herbs pre-cut at the grocery store, plan to first re-hydrate them in water when you get home before using them in your arrangements. Like all flower arrangements, change the water daily and pluck off leaves that are beginning to brown or wilt.

USE

Select an herb with a sturdy stem as a base and place them around the container on a diagonal, resting on the rim so that your herbs can lend structural support to your flowers. You can add softer stemmed herbs, like mint, later on to act as fillers and finishing touches.

CHOOSING CONTAINERS

Your imagination is the only limit when it comes to containers! Try to venture outside of the usual suspects; a unique vessel can add loads of impact. Often when we stop to assess our vase inventory we find many of the same shapes and sizes. While it's only natural to play favorites, relying on what is comfortable can take the life out of any hobby, causing a once-loved pursuit to become dull and monotonous. Be playful, bold, and take some risks!

SIZE & SHAPE

From tall, fluted vases to ceramic pedestal bowls and milk bottles, keep an open mind and experiment. In addition to varying the size of your vessels, consider the size of the openings at the top, because this dictates the size of your bouquet. You may love the more dramatic and full arrangements that you see in magazines, yet struggle when creating them at home and wonder why. It could be due to the opening at the top of your vase—so opt for one that is wider, such as a large, fluted ceramic variety. The opposite issue could be true; your vases all have very large openings so you feel forced to create big, blowsy bouquets (and spend lots of money!) whenever you make an arrangement. Eliminate this little problem by simply stocking vessels with smaller openings in your inventory. You can easily spray paint empty wine bottles (remove labels first and wash thoroughly) in a single color and pop in a pretty flower, arranging in a row along your credenza. Problem solved!

Outside of the opening, considering vessel height and width is also important when choosing your container. Low, wide vessels are perfect for coffee-table arrangements because you can still see over your flowers to watch television without moving the arrangement. Wide, round vessels look lovely when packed tightly with flowers that create an almost dome shape on top—carnations or roses look elegant when presented this way.

COLOR & TEXTURE

Break away from hard-and-fast color rules. Whether you opt to keep things understated, over-the-top, or somewhere in between, consider container color as you pull together your bouquet and think of the room in which you will place it. Containers that add some heat to an interior aren't always those that necessarily blend in magazine-perfect. If you like for everything to work harmoniously and match flawlessly, then by all means go for it. If not, and color doesn't come instinctively to you (most of us need help), grab a trusty color wheel (available at most craft stores and art shops) and work with tints and tones that lie closely together on the color wheel that are also in your space. Perhaps your living room is violet, beige, and green. By mixing in a broader variety of violets and greens in all of their tints and tones, from putty to jewel tones and even lime, your container could make some major impact to the overall scheme. Like everything else, the more you play and welcome the happy accidents, the easier it becomes to work with color.

Container texture is another worthy consideration when looking for the right vessel. Wood, stone, crackled glass, ridged or smooth vessels, or those with sparkle can quickly add flair to your flowers and give a definite style that can range from mid-century to country or coastal.

WEIGHT

You don't want to place your stunning cherry blossoms into a delicate lightweight vase only to see it topple over onto your table. When styling with branches or large blooms, look for a vase that is weighty and made from materials such as metal, thick glass, iron, or stone.

WATERPROOF—A MUST

Many of the most creative containers (wooden fruit crates, papier mâché pencil holders, vintage tins) are generally not watertight. No need to fear—that's what juice glasses and jam jars are for! We like to first arrange our bouquets in-hand, securing the stems with a rubber band to hold them in place, and then gently guide them into the watertight vessel ensuring all stems are submerged. Next, you can place the arrangement into the center of your container, which works best if the container is not transparent so you can hide your watertight vessel. Voilà! You've instantly solved what could have been a big puddle on your dining table.

TIED POSY ARRANGEMENT

you will need:
bud vase, a focal flower, six or seven secondary flowers in various colors and sizes, a ribbon

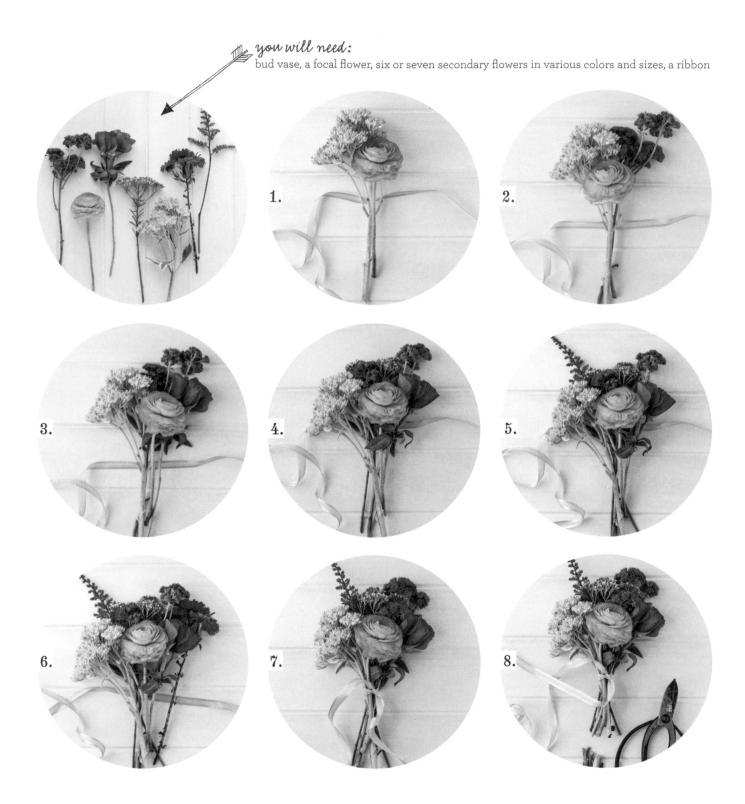

1. Start with your focal flower and pair it with a secondary flower that has a very different texture from your focal flower. This way the focal flower has a pretty backdrop texture next to it. In this arrangement we used a pale pink ranunculus paired with a pale white and pink sedum.

2. Next add some contrasting color that works well with your focal flower. We started with some purple-blue ageratum.

3. Continue to add in secondary flowers. We added magenta godetia next to the focal flower.

4. Bright pink asters and rice flowers build up the color story.

5. A delicate sprig of astilbe, longer than the other stems, adds height and varies the outline.

6. When you are happy with the posy gather the stems together.

7. Tie all the flowers together with a ribbon or some twine.

8. Trim the ends of the stems to the same length and then place in a pretty bud vase.

**FLOWERS USED
  IN THIS PROJECT:**
* Ranunculus
* Sedum
* Ageratum
* Godetia
* Aster
* Rice flower
* Astilbe

FLOWERS USED
   IN THIS PROJECT:
* Dahlia
* Chocolate mint
* Rosemary
* Lavender leaves
* Purple verbena
* Solidago
* Aster
* Queen Anne's lace

MEDIUM ARRANGEMENT WITH SASS

you will need:

your favorite container, a focal flower, a few sprigs of greenery, smaller secondary flowers in various textures and colors

method:

1. An easy approach to a medium-sized arrangement is to build it around a focal flower, in this case a two-toned dahlia. After cleaning and trimming all the flower stems, place the focal flower in your container.

2. Trim a few pieces of greenery to frame behind and around the focal flower as the fillers. We added chocolate mint first.

3. Further foliage fillers of rosemary and lavender leaves add contrasting gray tones.

4. Add in a smaller flower in a different color from the focal flower as your secondary flower. We first added purple verbena.

5. Then we added some yellow solidago (goldenrod). The solidago adds a fluffy texture to complement the round dahlia.

6. We then added some purple asters as they pick up the color of the verbena yet are different in size and texture. The yellow center of the aster works nicely with the solidago, too. Finally we added a filler of Queen Anne's lace to give this arrangement a natural just-picked-from-the-garden look.

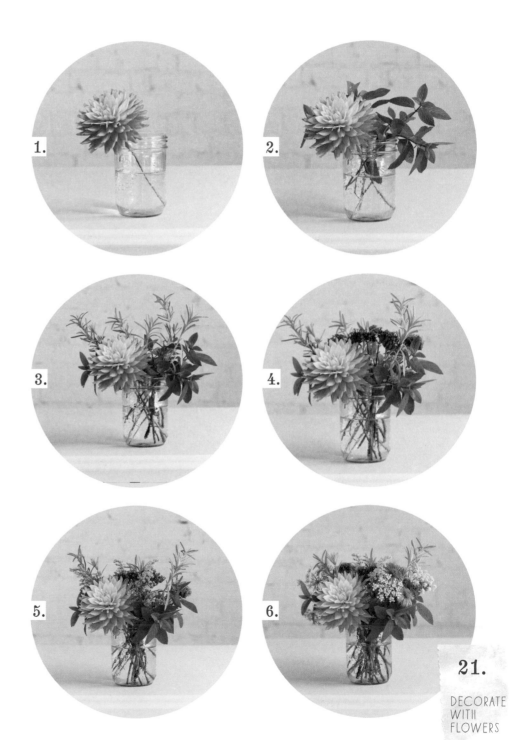

21.

DECORATE
WITH
FLOWERS

BIG BLOWSY ARRANGEMENT

you will need:
a large vase or container, various greens, three large focal flowers, five or six secondary flowers, a few smaller spray flowers for fillers

method:

1. When using a large container make sure that your greenery and flowers are tall enough. They should be a little taller than the height of the container. Of course, you can always break the rules, but their length should be at least one and two-thirds the height of the container or even double. You don't want your bouquet looking like it is being swallowed up by the vase! If you use greens first you can use fewer flowers—a great way to save money. We added a few types of green leaves, then some hydrangeas with their own leaves.

2. We added in some dark rusty Japanese maple leaves. Do not worry too much about structure— you want your flowers to look casual, as they do in the garden.

3. We then added some pale pink astrantia, which have small flower heads with a nice long stem.

4. Fragrant garden roses add color and the scent of the garden.

5. Finally a couple of poppies were placed in up high and a few magenta peonies a little lower.

6. Take a last look at the placement. For example, it is nice to allow the poppies to enjoy some space around them so their delicate petals catch the light.

FLOWERS USED
IN THIS PROJECT:
* Assorted green foliage
* Hydrangea
* Japanese maple leaves
* Astrantia
* Garden rose
* Poppy
* Peony

Chapter **1.** NATURAL

For lovers of a pure and simple decorating style, there are so many options for adding a gentle touch of fresh blooms and branches to your home without overdoing it or breaking the bank. The secret is to keep the look understated and try to strike a balance so that FRESH FLOWERS effortlessly fit into the room without overwhelming it. Natural style is casual, a breath of fresh air, with a definite focus on less being so much more.

We were inspired to create this scheme because the movement towards mindful living is one that we wholeheartedly embrace. Who doesn't delight in a cup of tea and toast on the terrace while listening to birdsong and feeling the garden breeze? It's these simple pleasures that make such a difference in our busy world. Natural style is all about finding the beauty in everyday things and making do with what you have.

Our natural style palette includes LUSH GREENS, SHADES OF WHITE AND CREAM, YELLOW, VIOLET, and BROWN because they are some of our favorites. We invite you to explore other colors that you feel a natural affinity towards that capture what this style means to you. Natural style should never look fussy, planned out, or stuffy, and because of that, it is one of the easiest looks to create. You don't need to spend much time creating effortless beauty. This is a great style to try if you are a beginner to flower arranging, because you can pluck pretty flowers and the more elegant looking weeds from your yard and use our tips for containers and for styling to make pretty floral displays for your home.

In this chapter, we'll show you how to turn a clothes hanger into a floral wreath, give tips on working with herbs, show you how to create a pressed flower book and a lush green wreath. We'll also share garland displays with bottles and another with tied-on blooms and weave in more imaginative ways to spruce up your interiors as we go. Finally, our relaxing dinner with friends just may inspire you to pull together an evening focused on the spirit of love and friendship.

Once you begin styling your flowers into vessels, use a light hand and work from the heart more than from what you think is right. In fact, play some of your favorite music and try not to think too hard. For instance, casually combine Queen Anne's lace and daisies in little jam jars wrapped with twine and add them down the center of your tabletop. Of course, certain occasions call for more elaborate presentations, such as a large party or wedding reception, but you have to start somewhere, so begin small and play with flowers at home.

No matter what the occasion, aim to keep it pared back and make your arrangements natural, welcoming, and, most of all, mix flowers that would naturally grow together in the wild. You likely won't find daisies and exotic orchids sharing a country field, so pairing them in a vase for this look wouldn't be the best natural combination.

UNDERSTATED, SIMPLE, PURE, RELAXED, NO FRILLS. Doesn't that sound like a style you can get behind?

27.

DECORATE
WITH
FLOWERS

A QUICK & SIMPLE WREATH

Create a wreath using a heavier-gauge floral wire to form a circle. Make a series of small bouquets or bunches out of greenery, wrapping the stems of each bouquet together with floral tape. Start at the top of the circle and attach the first bouquet to the wire form with more floral tape. Then work down one side, overlapping the next bouquet to cover the wrapped stems of the one before. When you get towards the bottom, start adding a couple focal flowers to your bouquets. Once you reach the bottom of the circle, start at the top and work down the other side. If needed, fill in any holes by adding a bloom or two using wire.

CREATE A PRETTY PRESSED FLOWER JOURNAL

Tape small clippings of favorite flowers and herbs onto acid-free watercolor paper and cover with another piece of paper, topping both with a heavy book. Leave small flowers for a couple weeks or until dry. Leaves and herbs may take a little longer. Large blooms can take four or more weeks. Use flowers at the peak of freshness for best results.

GLASS JAR LINE-UP

Little bottles and jars hold sprigs of edible flowers and herbs. Flowering chives, lavender, mint, and fennel can look pretty as a little posy in a mason jar. For color and style, line all of the bottles up on a window sill or on a shelf in your kitchen. Wrap jars with twine for an extra touch.

PAINTED TIN CAN

A simple two-tone bouquet can look beautiful, especially when you use lots of different textures. Here we combined mint and dogwood as our greenery, then mixed in chive flowers, lavender, and thalictrum for the filler flowers. Clematis blooms became our stunning focal flowers. A can painted with white latex paint made the perfect receptacle.

herbs for cooks
DECORATIVE AND LOVELY
TO USE IN COOKING OR
TEA-MAKING, FRESH HERBS
IN THE KITCHEN BRING A
NICE TOUCH OF WHIMSY
AND A GORGEOUS SCENT.

CALMING CHAMOMILE

Chamomile collected from the backyard and arranged into a ceramic pedestal vase is unexpected, yet striking and works beautifully on open shelving in the kitchen.

HANG THEM UP

Tiny bottles from the craft store are strung together using fine wire and hung to the wall on hooks to create an usual garland. This is a perfect way to show off tiny clippings of eucalyptus, thalictrum, lavender, and chive blossom. You can also decorate your bottles with washi tape or strips of fabric secured with ribbon, for additional pattern and color.

MEADOW CUTTINGS

A few fresh sprigs popped into a row of apothecary bottles from the flea market become an attractive display that brightens any corner. You can find flowers in your own garden that have that wildflower look, such as the flowering pea, astrantia, and fennel flowers we've used here. While some areas have laws limiting the clipping of certain wildflowers on public land, there is often no harm in grabbing a few pretty sprigs (especially the common "weedy" ones that grow in abundance) the next time you find yourself in the countryside.

FESTOONS OF FLOWERS & HERBS

You can easily string up a cheery festoon of flowers in little time and for mere pennies. Here we've collected vintage floral illustrations that were literally falling out of an antique botanicals book and taped them to the wall. To make the garland, simply secure your favorite flowers, herbs and other greenery, and some gift tags to a length of twine using 2-inch strips of string. You can make your festoons as long as you'd like, and you can add ribbon, strips of fabric, or anything else that you fancy as long as they're lightweight. Fix each end of your garland to the wall using a thumbtack or small nails. If you'd like to hide them, wrap a ribbon around each nail or tack, allowing it to trail down the wall a bit.

WE LOVE **CRASPEDIA**, ALSO CALLED **BILLY BUTTONS** DISPLAYED EITHER ALONE OR MIXED IN WITH FLORAL BOUQUETS. THESE LOVELIES ARE FLOWERING PLANTS IN **THE DAISY FAMILY KNOWN FOR THEIR GRAPHIC, SPHERICAL HEADS** AND CAN LIVE FOR UP TO TWO WEEKS AFTER THEY'VE BEEN CLIPPED. ONCE DRIED, YOU CAN KEEP THEM FOR SEVERAL MONTHS BEFORE THEY BEGIN TO LOSE THEIR VIVID COLOR.

A HAPPY YELLOW POP!

Entertaining ideas

The honest beauty of a simple spread, one that appears almost born rather than labored over, is something we value and appreciate immensely in a world that moves so quickly. Mingling over a warm comforting meal prepared with love transforms an evening, which may have been stressful if you'd opted for elaborate prep and process. Decadent parties are also a joy, but if you find yourself holding back from having guests because of the sheer work involved, a more natural approach may be the one for you.

When decorating your tabletop, please don't try too hard, and leave that fancy china and those delicate hand-painted vases in the cabinet. In fact, we've used what can be found in most homes—white ceramic dishware, plain glassware, understated linen placemats and napkins, and votive candles sitting on leaves plucked from the backyard.

SINGLE SPECIMENS

To recreate our natural style floral arrangements, try using jam jars and pop in a relaxed mix of flowers that are loosely arranged and seem to be gathered from a nearby meadow (even if they aren't!). We've used combinations of fennel flower, Queen Anne's lace, chive blossom, Japanese anemone, eucalyptus, verbena, mint, and dahlia. You can also add sprigs of fresh rosemary to your arrangements and then tie what's left to your napkins with a piece of twine. This is especially practical if what you've prepared in the kitchen is also with rosemary; it makes for a very nice touch and gives you the chance to use the entire bunch. You can personalize your jam jar arrangements with sweet greetings for your guests that also act as a place card. Wrap twine around the jar, handwrite your message on a basic tag, and secure the tag using a small wooden clothespin (or whatever you have on hand).

Step-by-step project

COAT HANGER WREATH

you will need:
wire coat hanger, floral tape, white spray paint, ribbon, scissors

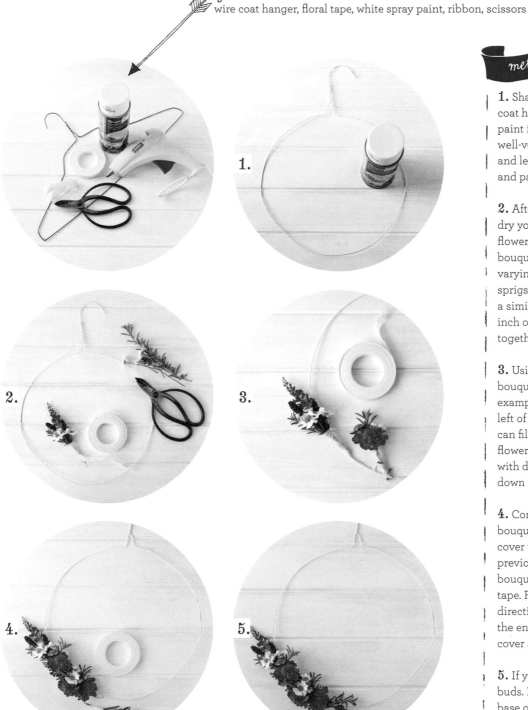

method:

1. Shape the bottom part of your coat hanger into a circle. Spray paint it white outdoors or in a very well-ventilated area. Paint one side and let it dry, before flipping over and painting the other side.

2. After the paint is completely dry you are ready to add the flowers. Make a very small bouquet using a few flowers in varying sizes, then add a couple sprigs of greenery. Trim stems to a similar size, leaving about an inch of stems. Wrap all the stems together with floral tape.

3. Using floral tape, wrap the bouquet to the hanger. In this example we went with the bottom left of the circle. If you like, you can fill the whole circle or add flowers only to the bottom center with delicate ribbons hanging down for a sweet finishing touch.

4. Continue making little bouquets and overlap them to cover the wrapped stems of the previous bouquet. Attach each bouquet to the hanger using floral tape. For the last bouquet flip the direction in order to finish off the end of the flower display and cover any wrapped stems.

5. If you spot gaps, collect a few buds. Push fine wire through the base of your buds, twist the wire, and attach the buds to the hanger.

37.

DECORATE
WITH
FLOWERS

FLOWERS USED IN THIS PROJECT:

✳ Lavender   ✳ Penstemon   ✳ Scabious   ✳ Daisy   ✳ Rosemary

chapter 2

PASTELS & NEONS

Pretty pastels morph into so much more when you add **A ZING OF FLUORESCENT PINK, LIME, ORANGE,** or **YELLOW** to the mix. We love pastels for their casual cool vibe and their obvious femininity and soft tones. Yet pastels can quickly become too sweet without neutrals, a little bling like copper and other metallics, and bright accents to ground them and bring in a bit of heat. Pastels and super-bright neons are enjoying a dynamic revival at the moment with the world of fashion mixing these two opposites, soft and spicy, so take cues from the runway and work them into your interiors through flowers.

For this look, we naturally selected some of our favorite pastel tones like **MINT, PALE PEACH, SOFT BLUE, BUTTER YELLOW,** and **PINK**. We also weaved in favorite neutrals like taupe and nude. We like to work with only one or maybe two neon accents so things don't become too busy or childlike and the eye knows where to look. You can also mix in deeper hues, like **APRICOT** or **TURQUOISE**, to give the palette a more sophisticated edge.

Pastels vary in depth and tone and punctuate a neutral scheme without dominating a space, making decorating possibilities endless. It's easy to go overboard though, so have the eye of an editor. Allow our ideas to inspire you, but definitely play with your own palette mixes since you'll likely find combinations that speak to your heart. We worked in bold, geometric and graphic patterns, for instance, to avoid pastel overkill.

If color isn't your strong point, don't fret—pick up a stack of paint swatches at the home store and move them around on a white surface, adding in neon ribbon to see what works together. Or cheat a little and grab a scarf with pastels and a hint of neon in the pattern and work from there.

When shopping for this look, you aren't likely to find neon fresh flowers unless they've been dyed and often those are super tacky, so you have to use your imagination when mixing neons into your arrangements by relying on how you dress up containers with accents, like ribbon, glass paint, or washi tape in neon hues.

Our hope is that these ideas will light your creative spark and help you get started as we share some of our favorite looks and introduce easy tips and tricks that you may not have considered before. We'll talk about edible flowers that can make for stunning finishing touches on food and we'll show very easy display ideas that add punch—like buds on cake stands, in glass vials, floating in bowls, and in painted tin cans (of all things!). You'll be invited to sit at our table for a midsummer's lunch and finally, we'll show you how to make chalky pastel jam jars.

This style is **DYNAMIC, FEMININE, FASHIONABLE,** and **FUN** but most of all, an opportunity to break out of a color rut and experiment with modern pastels in a new way by adding an edge!

41.

DECORATE
WITH
FLOWERS

Tie or glue a ribbon around the base of a small ceramic vase or a glass votive that you've decorated with latex paint to add your own individual flair.

Vary vessel shapes. A square or rectangular container can make a romantic bouquet look more sophisticated and modern. Don't be afraid to mix and match your shapes! Here we've combined circular bottles with a rectangular vase and used neon glass paint and white marker pens to create tiny patterns to tie them together.

Recycle a tin can from your kitchen with a few coats of latex or spray paint to complement your overall room scheme. Here we used plain white with our peonies and chrysanthemums, since we wanted the focus to be on the flowers, not the container.

Scatter several petite vases across a table, windowsill, or fireplace mantle and top each with a bold bloom. We kept our flowers cut close to the tops of the rim to show less stem and more of the romantic folds in these pretty petals of rose, poppy, peony, and chrysanthemum.

In Kate Horsman's Vancouver bedroom, the bold baroque silhouette of the Bourgie table lamp designed by Ferruccio Laviani for Kartell only needs a small arrangement of dahlias and tulips to add a subtle pocket of color and texture without disturbing this tranquil resting place.

Pastels are versatile and when paired with edgy brights (like neon) you can turn up the volume, giving them a forward, contemporary feel. Try tying the tops of your stems just under the blooms with long, flowing ribbons in fun brights to lend a festive touch, as shown in this array of snapdragon, larkspur, dusty miller, pittosporum, tulip, and astilbe.

WHO SAYS PASTELS CAN'T PACK A LITTLE PUNCH?

A few delicate blooms in even the simplest of vessels can add a dramatic statement to any room. Don't stress over crafting the perfect bouquet; often a stem, or a small bundle, is all that is needed. Also, consider placement and think of where flowers would make you the happiest? Would you enjoy them bedside to provide sweet dreams? What about on your desk to bring in a little nature? Could they be added to your entryway to greet you each day? If you don't think flowers add punch, place your hand over those shown in each image and imagine the same setting without them—not nearly as striking, right?

43.

DECORATE
WITH
FLOWERS

COLLECT & DISPLAY
LITTLE POCKETS OF CURATED INSPIRATIONS IN YOUR HOME TO CREATE VIGNETTES THAT MAKE YOU SMILE...

CURIOUS COLLECTION

We topped a table with pretty patterned paper that we cut and taped together to create a collage using fluorescent lime washi tape. You could even make your own placemats for your next kids' party this way. Next, we mixed assorted glasses and stemware, petite vintage tea saucers, and a cake stand to create our eclectic display of phlox, achillea, nerine, garden rose, peony, ranunculus, and white bluebell. On the wall, we used neon paint to highlight an illustration from a vintage floral book.

A FRESH TWIST

Moodboards in a work studio provide the perfect dose of creative inspiration. Have you thought to add fresh flowers to take them up a notch? You can use a petite, transparent flower vial, wrap a bit of wire around the top, pop in a single stem, and secure it to the wall using tape.

← ◄◄◄ **TIP**
Create mini cloche arrangements using glasses tipped upside down onto plates or saucers. Add a bit of water to hydrate, then place a pretty flower head (or two) and top with a glass. Note: Flowers require fresh air to avoid wilting, so we recommend this look for short-term projects, such as when you're expecting guests, or opt for silk or paper flowers.

45.

DECORATE WITH FLOWERS

TIP Add floating candles to your arrangement or place sequins, pebbles, or crystals like quartz and pyrite in the bottom of your bowl, for a little shimmer and shine.

FLOWERS AFLOAT

Shallow, ceramic bowls are transformed into a must-try centerpiece when filled with fragrant blooms and herbs (we love mint!). Wide flat flowers such as orchids, asters, gerbera daisies, gardenias, and open roses won't sink as quickly as those with heavier centers, which can sink within an hour. To give pastels a kick, introduce almost-fluorescent pops of blooms, like fresh pink geranium and bright lime hydrangea.

SPARKLE SPARKLE!

A white ceramic platter was transformed into a sparkling centerpiece by using tea lights wrapped with patterned washi tape, silver sequins, and dried straw flowers. Charming!

FANCIFUL FOODS

If you don't have time to bake a cake for your daughter's birthday, or if you're just not a baker, customize a store-bought cake with fresh flowers. You'll want to garnish with non-toxic flower heads, so speak with your florist to inquire about the best blooms to use. We used garden roses, geranium, lavender, and dianthus and tied ribbon to the base of our cake stand for an extra dose of color.

NON-TOXIC FLOWER VARIETIES

All non-toxic flowers need to be certified organic or grown sustainably if they are to come in contact with food since chemical herbicides or pesticides found in non-organic flowers can make even non-toxic flowers problematic. Next, remove pistils and stamens (pollen-bearing parts) on your edible flowers before use since some people have allergic reactions to pollen and it can also trigger asthma. For a list of our favorite common edible blooms, see the flower favorites on page 140.

PERSONAL TOUCHES MAKE IT SPECIAL

A sprig of dusty miller, with its textured, silvery leaves, is the perfect muted accent when tied onto a creamy white napkin with neon pink cord. Skip placemats and tablecloths for this look and think casual. Sprinkle the table with handmade confetti that you can make with a medium-sized circle punch found at most craft stores. We went with white for a bit of contrast against the rustic wooden table, but you can punch circles using patterned or solid papers in your favorite pastel or neon hues, depending on what works with the surface of your table.

Entertaining ideas

TAKE YOUR SEATS FOR A MIDSUMMER LUNCH

Gather your girlfriends for a midsummer lunch! A palette of soft pastels accented with hints of neon is total eye candy that feels fresh and energetic. Twinkle lights strung across a white piano lend a casual touch and a bit of warmth. Our choice is to purchase those with a white cord because they seem to blend more easily into most room schemes. They may be a bit harder to find than the green variety so source them online instead. A variety of floral arrangements in all sizes are proof that the typical "flowers in the center of a table" look isn't the only way to go. We displayed single stems in tiny glasses down the center and at the far end placed a medium and large arrangement to create a focal point as guests enter the space. Large arrangements in the center of a table can make it hard to see your friends, so try this idea the next time you want to include blooms that are large and in charge!

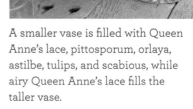

A smaller vase is filled with Queen Anne's lace, pittosporum, orlaya, astilbe, tulips, and scabious, while airy Queen Anne's lace fills the taller vase.

1.

2.

3.

4.

method:

1. Hardware stores often sell small sample-size containers of latex paint. This is an inexpensive way to get a wide variety of colors for this project as you do not need much paint for each jar. Pour a small amount of paint into a clean glass jar.

2. Coat the inside of the jar by tilting it to move the paint around as you cover the inside. Add more paint as needed.

3. When the inside is fully coated, carefully pour out any excess paint and wipe the rim and outside of the jar clean. Let dry. This may take a day or two.

4. You cannot get the inside of your painted jars wet as the paint will peel off, so place smaller bottles inside to hold the water for your flowers.

FLOWERS USED IN
THIS PROJECT:
* Garden rose
* Lavender
* Dahlia

Chapter ③. MARKET

x x x x x x x x

When we visit large bustling cities like London, Paris, and New York, we delight in exploring the bevy of vibrant outdoor markets to surround ourselves with the sights and sounds of local culture. Our travels inspired this look, because market style is about the art of being a magpie through unearthing hidden treasures in order to locate something endearing. It's about tapping into all of your senses and allowing your eclectic, quirky spirit to soar. Surprisingly, it also captures some elements of natural style, since it is also quite un-fussy, so it's a fitting approach to try if you feel more color courage and want to turn up the volume.

Our colors of choice for this look fell naturally into a lively palette that fits the typical market scene with various tones of **RED, YELLOW, VIOLET, PINK,** and **BLUE**. While we provide basic color recipes for each style in this book, we encourage you to try your own combinations according to what works with your room scheme at home.

This look requires imagination because it's all about doing things a bit unconventionally and stepping outside of tradition. As you shop street markets, pay special attention to vendor displays and notice how imaginative they are when it comes to attracting attention to their wares and repurposing objects. The same goes with styling flowers for this look at home—you'll want to think outside of what's typical to add a little pep. Plopping flowers into a vase may work for a more minimalistic look, but we're not going for standard fare here, so see where your imagination takes you. Look at everything in your home and ask: Can I use this to hold flowers? If not, can I tweak it? A row of glass vials from the craft store can be, with a bit of wire, quickly transformed into the prettiest of delicate vases to hang from the wall topped with the perfect bloom of fresh hydrangea in each. Tie a few vintage ribbons to your vials and boom! You've captured a little market style.

In our discussion of market style, we'll show you how to repurpose vessels, set a table for a charming market brunch with friends, use fabric on plant pots, create wall cones and a very clever display or two with bunches of bottles along with other creative ideas. We'll also talk about how we approached styling the rooms in this section so you can walk away with some decorating tips, too.

CHARMING, BUSY, INSPIRATIONAL, COLORFUL, NOSTALGIC, ZESTY... How can you not identify with some elements of this look?

55.

DECORATE
WITH
FLOWERS

Arrange smaller bouquets into shorter cylindrical vessels (like cans) by applying a looser dome-like effect. Keep your focal flowers higher and gradually add filler flowers, with the lowest blooms resting their heads on the rim.

Coordinate your bouquet style with your vessel. A casual container with laid-back blooms can result in perfectly imperfect bliss.

COLOR & PATTERN KA-POW!

Visit a grocery store for a little market style and look for canned fruits and teas, since they often have delightful color and pattern-filled containers. Best part is, they're affordable and can be easily washed and recycled after you've enjoyed their contents—a snack and a vase all-in-one!

To avoid rust or leaks, put small glasses inside your cans to hold flowers.

Throwing a party or planning a special dinner? Decorate your space for just a day using fresh flowers and washi tape. We love washi tape because it's safe for most surfaces and easy to use. Post soirée, you can clip off flower heads and float in shallow bowls filled with water (see page 47) to enjoy their beauty longer.

FLOWERS TAPED TO THE WALL? YES, PLEASE!

Tip: This idea works with faux flowers too, so experiment with different papers or the silk variety to see what fantastic displays you can create!

57.

PLAYING IT SAFE IS A DRAG. UNEXPECTED DISPLAYS AND BRIGHT BURSTS OF COLOR ADD HEALTHY TENSION AND PERSONALITY!

WALL CONES
These cute cones can be made simply by rolling brightly patterned paper and fixing with tape. Trim the top of the cone edge with sharp scissors. Give tiny posies water by wrapping stems in a little wet tissue and plastic wrap, then close the wrap around the stems with an elastic band. Place the posies into the cones and tape to the wall with paint-friendly tape. Alternatively, lay a cone on each plate at your next dinner party. Or use them to bring as hostess gifts or a thank you gift.

LIFT YOUR SURFACES
A heavy concrete shelf (above) is made instantly lighter with hydrangea blooms in a glass vase. Color is brought to a marble table top (left) with bright ranunculus and a vase of magenta waxflowers. A ranunculus is perched on a wooden pedestal beneath a glass dome. This is a way of enjoying a bloom that has fallen from its stem.

POPPING PATTERN

Instead of doing the predictable and matching the flowers exactly to this fabulous sofa in Joanna Fletcher's Vancouver home, we decided to have some fun and show that bright lively colored flowers in various tints and tones can work too. On the table we used bright pink ranunculus and creamy yarrow to work with the sofa and to complement our wall cones, then mixed in orange roses, magenta waxflowers, and yellow tulips. Flowers offer a temporary fix for times when you want to introduce bright colors that you may not want in the room all of the time.

ON A BUDGET? EXPRESS YOUR CREATIVITY WITH INEXPENSIVE GLASS BOTTLES AND VINTAGE BOTANICAL POSTCARDS FROM THE FLEA MARKET.

BOTTLE CHANDELIER

A bottle chandelier can be made out of a wire loop, heavy-gauge florist wire, lighter-gauge florist wire, and vintage or interesting small glass bottles. You will need to hang it securely from the ceiling with a hook. Use light wire to wrap around the necks of the bottles (this only works if there is a rim to hold the wire below) then attach the other end of the wire to the loop frame. Attach your bottles at varying lengths and space them evenly around the wire loop for balance. Use as little water as possible in the bottles and pop a flower or two into each one.

Tip: Play dress up! Tie ribbons in several lengths and colors to your loop for a festive touch.

STYLISH CHAIRBACKS

Use light-gauge florist wire for strength, versus twine, and tie one flower-filled vintage bottle at a time to the back of a chair. Use various shapes, sizes, and colors (we've mixed pale blue with clear), with different lengths of wire to create the perfect party accent on a special day of celebration. Add ribbons for even more pizzazz!

COFFEE TABLE COLOR BOOST

Having two colors that tie the arrangement to the rest of the room décor lets you pull in an array of other colors while still making the flowers look like they belong. In this case the bright pink ranunculus and the creamy colored yarrow coordinate with the throw pillow as well as the facing sofa shown on page 59. The addition of orange, yellow, and purple provides an element of surprise and shows that you need not limit your color palette.

STRING OF FLOWERS

A pretty garland of silk flowers can be made quickly by securing the stems to your string with ribbons and pieces of fabric. For special occasions dress up your garland by adding a few fresh flowers like roses, freesia, and lavender for a scented display.

FLOWERS ELEVATE YOUR SPACE AND YOUR MOOD. THESE NOOKS WOULDN'T BE THE SAME WITHOUT THESE FANTASTIC FLORAL TOUCHES.

Entertaining ideas

MARKET BRUNCH
WITH FRIENDS

Think cheerful, welcoming, and vibrant—just like your local outdoor market! Setting a market-style table is all about creating an atmosphere for guests and requires only a wee bit of decorating prep, yet delivers a feel-good setting. For a touch of charm, mix in dainty floral prints through your choice of napkins or other table linens. Introduce brightly-colored glassware to group small fresh floral arrangements in different color mixes so your bouquets mimic those found in bins at the market—varied and bright! We've mingled yellow tulips with craspedia and yarrow, orange ranunculus and roses with purple veronica and pink roses, and corn flowers with creamy white alstroemeria.

HANDMADE WITH LOVE

Add a handmade, crafty touch by topping a floral napkin with faux leaves and a fresh fragrant rose, then secure with ribbon. We love the floral prints and patterns by Liberty London and always stock up on a yard or two whenever we can. You can easily turn fabric into napkins, or use it to cover pots (see page 67 for how to do this).

DO IT YOUR WAY

Attention to detail when entertaining makes a huge impact, so think of the story you are trying to communicate to your guests, add in personal touches, and let instinct be your guide. While we hope our different entertaining ideas serve as inspiration and motivation to try new ideas, we encourage you to look at how you can translate our vision to suit your personal style. For instance, for our market brunch, you may want to introduce a natural linen tablecloth with napkins and placemats made from Liberty fabrics along with a pop of neon ribbon around your napkins, pretty place cards, and top it all off by suspending strands of ribbon from the backs of your chairs.

FLOWERS USED
   IN THIS PROJECT:
* Dahlia
* Japanese anemone
* Queen Anne's lace
* White nigella
* Garden rose
* Zinnia
* Aster
* Phlox

terra cotta plant pot and tray, sponge brush, Mod Podge, cotton floral fabric (we used Liberty prints), scissors, white spray paint (optional), glass jars

method:

1. If your fabric is thin you may want to spray paint your pot white; otherwise the orange might show through. Let it dry. Cut your fabric to a size that can easily wrap your pot, leaving at least an inch and a half above the rim of the pot and enough to cover the bottom. Apply Mod Podge to a small area of the pot and press the fabric down, applying more to the fabric with your sponge brush as you go.

2. Work in small areas, starting at the top rim and working down and around the pot in one direction. Apply Mod Podge to both the pot and the inner side of the fabric. Gently pull the fabric smooth as you go. Work quickly as the Mod Podge dries quite fast.

3. Once the surface is covered with fabric, apply Mod Podge beneath the fabric at the top and tuck it inside your pot. Repeat this process on the bottom of your pot, too. Apply Mod Podge all over the outer side of the fabric.

4. Let your pot dry on a piece of plastic and then follow a similar process for the bottom tray. Use little jars to hold the water for your flowers in the pots.

Chapter **4.** HAPPY BRIGHTS

Decorating with bright colors requires a certain amount of fearlessness, doesn't it? We love **AN ENERGETIC PALETTE WITH PLENTY OF BRIGHT STROKES** and decided that **HAPPY BRIGHTS** would encourage those who love color but are a bit shy when it comes to using it at home. Primary hues are often relegated to children's bedrooms and play areas. The rooms in this chapter prove that bold brights need not be childish. In fact, we'll show you exactly how to inject your space with brilliant primaries for very grown-up and radiant results.

For this section, we're mixing mostly bold primary hues with a few strategic pops of objects with retro touches and geometric prints, along with lots of clean lines and smooth, shiny surfaces. Together they all serve to lend pattern and texture to a home, but also work for those with a clean, modern decorating sensibility. We'll show you how to transform a nondescript white cabinet into a fabulous focal point by combining flowers with decorative objects that you most likely already own. We'll also give you plenty of tips on how we **USE FLOWERS TO ECHO THE COLOR POPS IN A SPACE TO CREATE VISUAL HARMONY** by experimenting in small ways.

In this section, we work with gerbera daisies, dahlias, zinnias, solidago, and yellow spray chrysanthemums. We enjoy highlighting the more ordinary and easy-to-find flowers because one thing that frustrates us when we find fabulous arrangements in our favorite books is that they can be difficult to replicate without spending a lot of money and having to place a custom order. Unless we're planning a wedding or special event, we don't want to invest so much time and expense into the flowers that we work with. You may have an entirely different approach, but we like to focus on what's available and seasonal to create a little magic, and hope we can inspire you to do the same.

For our DIY project, we'll show you how to make your own craspedia (billy buttons) to **ADD SOME GRAPHIC FUN TO YOUR ARRANGEMENTS**, along with a vase you can make in seconds using your favorite gift wrap. For entertaining, we've crafted a low key but lovely kids' party that you can pull together in a snap and the best part is our flower displays can be created before guests arrive—kids often love to work on creative projects and to be part of the prep.

Vibrant, geometric, playful, unexpected, retro, clean, and bright—we hope that you enjoy our ideas on how to infuse your interiors with some oomph factor through happy blooms!

71.

DECORATE
WITH
FLOWERS

Children's rooms should reflect their personality and style, so encourage them to decorate early on. They can experiment first by creating small vignettes until they feel confident enough to select their own bedding and wallpaper later on. Most kids delight in picking their own bouquets from the yard or flower shop and working with you to make pretty arrangements together—it can feel so "grown up" and fun!

Display what brings you joy by keeping your collections front and center on open shelves, windowsills, and dresser tops. Adding color to a windowsill makes even the gloomiest day feel more positive and bright. In a happy home, add bright stems to shiny vases in bold hues to make your styling sing! We love adding flowers alongside books and decorative objects to bring in a bit of nature and to add a sculptural element.

Create your own happy place in a bedroom that packs some punch. Some of the best ideas in the home are often the simplest; like the addition of flowers to your bedside table. Share the love and treat your companion to a petite fresh bouquet, too. Orange is an inspiring, zesty hue to wake up to and can really energize. Of course, your flowers need to work with your room scheme, so consider that before plucking your favorite stems.

Isn't this vase the best? Place flowers in decorative and quirky vessels that fit their personality. A yellow tulip may not have looked as beautiful as these bold dahlias with their spiky petals mimicking the motif on this shiny pale blue vase.

BRIGHT COLORS & CHEERFUL PATTERNS
MAKE YOU HAPPY!

Enliven the everyday. Vancouver-based interior designer Nancy Riesco has bright bursts of color and pattern, varying scale and texture to lend depth and flair. We love colorful accessories set against a neutral background, in this case pure white. You can change up your palette on a whim with colorful accessories.

Think of your home as a canvas, a continual art project; a very personal painting that is unique to you and your family. With a neutral base, coupled with pale wood tones, you're able to ground the space, giving rooms a sense of harmony and flow. Of course, there is no need to fear wallpaper and colorfully painted surfaces. In fact, if you want to add color to your walls, doors, floors, and ceilings, then by all means follow your heart. Just remember to add flowers for the perfect finishing touch! It's not hard to make the mundane amazing. Most think of white walls and white furniture as sterile or boring. The rooms shown in this section are neither, due to their clever use of color, texture, objects, and their placement, along with fresh flowers. What could have been ho-hum has loads of fire and punch.

AMPLIFY YOUR ART

Dedicated wall space for art, known as a gallery or focal wall, is very common in homes these days because collecting multiple pieces to build a stunning collection over time is enjoyable and packs visual punch. If you have a credenza, table, or floating shelf nearby, the addition of flowers can really accentuate your artwork. Select a few colors in your art collection that you want to enhance. Here, we worked with eight vases, grouped to form only three distinct areas where your eye lands as it travels, first from the cake stand display to the small pink bud vase and finally to the green glass vase, making a multitude of containers feel unified and not cluttered.

By placing the flowers to the left, the bold red "2" takes prominence without competing, as it would have if they'd been centered on the credenza or placed to the right.

Arrange an eclectic bunch of vases together on a tray or cake stand to unify the collection. If you want to get creative and play with height, tip sturdier vessels upside down and add smaller vases on top. This is a great trick if all of your vases are the same height.

PLAY WITH SCALE BY PLACING VASES ON TOP OF BOOKS, CAKE STANDS, BOXES, OR ANYTHING ELSE DECORATIVE SO YOUR FLOWERS TAKE ON NEW HEIGHTS.

DECORATE WITH FLOWERS

CREATE HARMONY

Look for ways to tie your flowers and containers in with your surroundings. The blue and green toned glassware complements the peacock blue cushion, knit pouf, and the pale blue rug. Fuchsia, red, and purple dahlias along with a zinnia highlight the bold and beautiful cashmere sofa throw. Bold colors in neutral spaces look fantastic when artfully grouped into key spots so a room doesn't become too busy. Clusters of color placed in different parts of the room allow the eye to travel, which adds to the overall appeal.

AS YOU ARRANGE FLOWERS & VASES, STEP BACK EVERY FEW MOMENTS TO VIEW YOUR COMPOSITION AS A WHOLE TO SEE IF YOU NEED TO ADD, OR TAKE AWAY, ANYTHING.

SUPPORTING ROLE

Flowers are not always meant to be the shining stars of a room; in fact they're often in the role of supporting actor. This is particularly important to consider when styling them next to a very prominent object in your room—like a bold painting. The goal is to highlight it, not overpower with a massive arrangement. To avoid flowers competing with interiors, consider a less-is-more approach. This spiky dahlia sits artfully in a ceramic bowl on a wooden tray topping a George Nelson platform bench; all work with the painting, not against it.

FIND A COMMON LINK,
TELL YOUR OWN INTERIOR STORY,
& CREATE WARMTH AND MEANING.

SIMPLE SNIPS

Snip a bloom with a dome shape (rather than flat) in a similar size to this spiky dahlia. Trim the stem 1 to 2 inches from the head and add water to a bowl around the same diameter as your flower. Rice bowls work well with their narrow bottoms and wide tops and can be found almost anywhere. Other flower heads that fit perfectly into a rice bowl: lotus, peony, allium, English rose, hydrangea.

KIDS' PARTY TIME!

Kids' parties give you the chance to let your imagination run wild so enjoy experimenting with some of those DIY ideas you've been dying to execute! Take a clean approach to your table setting, leaving plenty of space for the food. We've gone simple and affordable without sacrificing style. In fact, you can make these containers in less than 15 minutes with supplies kids typically use for their own creative ideas, and find the flowers at the grocery store. A favorite trick employed by stylists is to group ordinary blooms like carnations, daisies, and gerberas so the focus is on the color and not the flower type.

Entertaining ideas

STAMP IT!

Arrangements and containers need not be elaborate to make children feel special and to look stunning in the photos you'll likely be snapping. We've selected yellow spray chrysanthemums and solidago and placed them in white coffee cups decorated with blue stars that were applied using a rubber stamp. Tip: Put a handful of stones or a rock in the bottom of each paper cup to add weight so it won't easily topple over.

FLOWERS TO GO

While place cards are helpful for formal events, they're not required here (often kids won't sit where you tell them to anyway!) so put the extra effort into something more rewarding, like party favors, sweetly decorated cupcakes, and take-away flower arrangements. Try this easy DIY: Place party favor bags over glass bottles and tie with a ribbon, adding in a sweet bouquet. Allow your little guests to take them home for their parents—always a sweet gesture.

This table is set and ready for its young guests. A palette of bright primary colors adds a definite "wow" factor to a kids' party, whether it be a post-sleepover brunch or a more planned-out birthday celebration. We've selected fresh yellow, orange, and blue primary hues, with hints of spring green, and mixed in playful graphic patterns in polka dots, stars, and chevron prints. This mix is youthful and fun without clashing with the rest of the space.

79.

DECORATE
WITH
FLOWERS

Step-by-step project
PAPER VASE
& WOODEN CRASPEDIA

you will need:

wooden beads, wooden dowels to fit bead hole diameter, yellow acrylic paint, craft glue, paint brush, craft knife, paper cup, patterned paper, rectangular glass vase

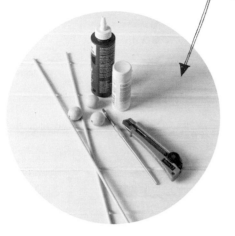

method:

1. Apply glue to the end of a dowel and then stick the bead on. Allow to dry.

2. Apply paint to the bead and allow to dry. Apply another coat to get good coverage, then allow to dry. Trim the other end of the dowel with your craft knife to the desired length.

3. Measure all sides of your vase and trim your paper to fit. Then create clean folds in the paper that will fit snugly into the corners of your vase.

4. Place the folded paper in your vase and then add a paper cup in the center to hold the water for your bouquet. After arranging your flowers, pop in your craspedia and you're finished!

1.

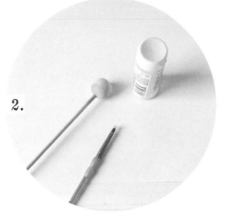

2.

FLOWERS USED
   IN THIS PROJECT:
* Dahlia
* Zinnia

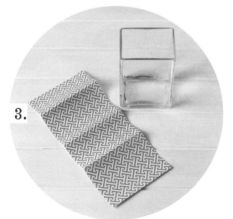

3.

4.

Chapter 5. COASTAL

Who doesn't love a visit to the coast? We were both raised beachside so leaving coastal style out of our book was inconceivable. This look is versatile, laid back, light, natural and the color palette is perfectly sublime. Even if you live a thousand miles away from the sea, coastal style also contains certain elements that you can pull in without looking out of place or tacky. A cottage in the country can work with **WEATHERED WOODS, BLUE AND GREEN TONES, PALE-PAINTED FLOORBOARDS,** and **FLORAL WREATHS**.

As children, memories of our beach visits with family and friends are some of our fondest. Who doesn't love collecting shells, building a fire, snacking on fish and chips, and making sandcastles? The idea of merging some of our early childhood inspirations with our favorite memories of the shore as adults to create a clean, modern, and sun-kissed sensibility was an exciting concept. We quickly realized though that it's not easy to create coastal-inspired looks without things becoming very theme-y or looking like something from a tourist's gift shop! We really enjoyed creating a coastal style of our very own that is far from tacky.

Our coastal palette works with mostly **TONES OF WHITE** and **CREAM, BLUE,** and **YELLOW WITH HINTS OF VERY SOFT SEASHELL PINK**. We've used mostly white-washed and weathered woods, ceramic and glass vases,

and some unexpected patterns to keep this look very easy-breezy, carefully treading the waters to avoid the typical nautical themes of sailboats and stripes. We envisioned more of the South Carolina shoreline, pale and bright, over the dark waters and rocky coasts of the north for this look, so you won't find many deep blues, greens, or grays, though that is certainly another direction you could take if you love to envelop yourself in deeper hues. If deep blues, grays, and greens, like emerald and putty and indigo, more closely resemble what coastal style means to you, then apply your palette to our ideas. If you're not already a fan of coastal style then we hope this chapter will give you a fresh perspective and provide you with practical decorating and DIY ideas.

We will show you how to incorporate graphic, geometric, and tiny floral patterns to enhance a space. We'll share many affordable options for getting creative using things you may already have, like branches, glass bottles, paint, and cloches. You will also be invited to attend a beachy brunch with designer Rachel Ashwell in her coastal home in LA. Finally, we'll demonstrate how to whip up a quick and easy DIY container using twine and string.

EASY, BREEZY, SUN-KISSED, and **SERENE** ... Pull up a deck chair and pop an umbrella into your favorite cocktail—we're going coastal!

85.

DECORATE
WITH
FLOWERS

TALL AND ELEGANT

When you have enormous heavy blooms like these dahlias it can be more than enough to group them together without adding anything else. Keeping the stems long, we placed them in a crackled glass vase for an effortless and airy look.

WORK'S A BREEZE

The barely-peach dahlias add a
warm seashell tone to this bright
breezy office. Whether the
arrangement is an extravagant
bouquet or just a single stem,
an office is a wonderful place
to enjoy flowers. A fresh flower
can wake up a desk area and
provide some visual relief from
the stacks of paper and our
computer screens.

CONTRAST OF TEXTURE

When you have a striking piece of art, like this photograph by Hilda Grahnat above a built-in shelving system by San Francisco–based craftsman Michael Woo, there is no need to compete with your flowers. We opted for textural contrasts in our selection of blooms and a little shine with glass cloches. In the first cloche, we've arranged scabious together with a bit of gomphrena, some perky euphorbia beneath the second, and a single stem of spiky chrysanthemum in a simple juice glass.

FEEL AT HOME IN A SERENE INTERIOR PEPPERED WITH SOFT FLOWERY ACCENTS THAT SOOTHE AND BRING YOUR HEART PEACE.

UNEXPECTED SURPRISES

Have you ever thought to add flowers to handles and doorknobs? This is a great display idea for cabinets and doors that are used infrequently, like those shown on this weathered wooden china cabinet. You can create mini wreaths and garlands, find a hanging container, or create your own using a jam jar and wire (see decoratewithflowers.com for this project). In this small arrangement we've used a mix of white scabious, Queen Anne's lace, white statice, yellow spray rose, solidago, anthemis, garland chrysanthemum, white waxflower, and borage as the texture, shape, and color fit a sunny coastal scheme quite beautifully.

WORK WITH WHAT YOU HAVE

Many think that you have to go overboard with flowers to create the most impact. We disagree and often find the organic, less formal arrangements to be the most inspiring and from the heart. In this line up, the natural light inspired us to go with clear glass milk bottles and wispy, textural stems of white alstroemeria, fennel flower, agapanthus, craspedia, and baby's breath to keep the look light and fresh, just like a day at the shore.

WEATHERED WOOD TAKES US IMMEDIATELY TO THE COAST.

This cabinet with its peeling soft blue paint is reminiscent of pretty painted cottages that have been sprayed with salt water and wind again and again. Its small door knob provides a hanging place for a coat hanger wreath, which you can easily make yourself as shown on pages 36–37. A few pieces of greenery and some cream and yellow flowers work well together to create an easy yet unique floral display.

WILLOW WARE

Collections of ceramic vessels can bring color and pattern, as in the home of Victoria artist Kate Campbell. Fill one of the pieces with white and cream colored flowers like alstroemeria, lysianthus, scabious, lysimachia, and Queen Anne's lace. Add a few blue focal flowers like these hydrangeas, or try delphiniums, blue bonnets, cornflowers, or agapanthus.

bright blue bursts

A serene white bedroom with wooden shutters looks fresh and inviting with a white water jug filled with hydrangea blooms. Hydrangeas are unscented and do not usually aggravate those with allergies. They are a perfect choice for a guest bedroom!

IDEAS FOR DISPLAYING PATTERN

If you have a lot of pattern in a room why not add a punch of color with just one type of flower among a mix? Here the bright sunny yellow of the dahlias gives a pop of color against all the blue and white pattern. A few blue delphiniums and a white hydrangea provide texture and interest without making the overall floral display too busy.

UPCYCLED CONTAINERS

Some jars and bottles from the recycle bin are given a coat of white flat spray paint. When dry we added acyclic paint in varying blue tones for a gradient effect. This is an easy way to add a little coastal vibe in any room. Just remember the paint is not waterproof, so be careful pouring water in and out of the bottles.

DON'T BE AFRAID TO MIX AND MATCH LOTS OF PATTERNS TOGETHER IN A ROOM. JUST KEEP THE COLOR PALETTE THE SAME TO AVOID VISUAL OVERLOAD.

HOOPLA!

An easy way to decorate a wall with loads of pattern is by using embroidery hoops to showcase your favorite fabrics. Keeping the palette contained, such as just blues, makes it even more graphic.

BRANCHING OUT

A few small lightweight glass vases hang from wire loops on a spray-painted branch. Make sure you put the branch in a heavy vase so that it does not tip over. Choose flowers in the same color for a simpler look.

93.

DECORATE
WITH
FLOWERS

WE INVITE YOU TO JOIN US FOR A BEACHY BRUNCH!

When we thought about how the typical brunch comes together—often rather spontaneously—we decided to work with what was readily available in this space to create something special. If you don't have flowers on hand, you can pluck what you have from the garden or deconstruct a larger arrangement that may be elsewhere in the home to turn it into something new. We kept our five compact arrangements low so guests can easily mingle among a calming scheme of blue and white, and added in lots of leafy greens for a dose of texture, color, and to provide contrast in the crisp white space. Spotless linen napkins and a mix of polished glassware plus white porcelain bowls and plates equal relaxed simplicity at its best.

FLOWER STORIES

It's typical when selecting flowers for your home to consider form, texture, contrast, color, scale, and proportion, but don't forget the importance of creating an overall atmosphere. What distinctive qualities about a time or place are you trying to recreate through your flowers and how can your choices accomplish

this? Our perky clusters provide lots of texture that mimics the natural life found by the sea. The spidery blooms of white nerine, spiky blue delphinium, and eryngium with its spiny leaves remind us of starfish, while the seeded eucalyptus with its droopy pale leaves and seed pods has an almost seaweed-like characteristic. To add in something that resembles sea grass, we've chosen *Panicum* 'Frosted Explosion' with its airy plumes that seem to sway in the breeze.

SEASIDE WHITES

Guests are encouraged to relax and feel completely at home in this charming seaside dining room belonging to designer Rachel Ashwell. White in its various tones, along with rustic and whitewashed woods, creates a pure, relaxed interior space with definite coastal charm. A white oak farmhouse table in a distressed antique white finish combined with versatile chairs make this space an unfussy and peaceful coastal retreat.

95.

DECORATE
WITH
FLOWERS

FLOWERS USED
  IN THIS PROJECT:
* Dahlia
* Japanese anemone
* Fennel flower
* Queen Anne's lace
* White statice
* White scabious
* Garland daisy

you will need:

clean recycled jars or bottles, craft glue, glue gun, string in various colors, scissors, sponge brush

method:

1. Apply a small dab of glue from a glue gun at the top of the jar just below the lid ridge. Carefully attach string to the glue and allow to dry. Please be careful when using hot glue.

2. Once dry, apply craft glue around the top quarter of the jar and begin wrapping your string snugly around it. Apply more craft glue to cover about two thirds of the jar. Continue wrapping with string.

3. Once two thirds of your jar is covered by wrapped string, cut the string and carefully secure with a dab of hot glue. Next, alternate your string by adding a different color or texture by placing the starting end in the dab of hot glue where the last string finished.

4. Follow the process of starting and finishing with new string as you go until you've covered the final third of the jar. Finish at the bottom with another dab of hot glue to secure the end in place. Use as many different colors as you like or cover your jar in only one color—it's up to you!

Chapter **6.** NEUTRAL POP

Neutral pop combines mostly **BEIGE TONES** with **VIOLETS** for a contemporary and classy mood. Beige is often dubbed as "safe" and purple as "shocking" but the truth is that both colors are surprisingly diverse and versatile, looking particularly gorgeous when paired because beige neutralizes stronger colors to bring harmony to a palette. In this section, we focus on beige as our neutral though gray would be another terrific option. In fact, any neutral can be revved up with a jolt of peppy color!

Beige is a very pale brown known for its warm appearance. **PURPLE (OR VIOLET) CAN RANGE FROM A SOFT, POWDERY LILAC TO SMOKY WINE AND VIBRANT FUCHSIA.** If you worry about combining the two, think about cosmetics and how stunning your neutral foundation can look with smoky purple eyes and a deep wine lip color—gorgeous. If you're not already experimenting with beige or purple then these pages may give you a nudge of inspiration and a huge dose of happy!

For this section, we wanted to challenge ourselves and work with both beige and violet to present a fresh interpretation on how to work with colors that have a strong contrast without compromising style. This style is a little out of our comfort zone and in our professions, we need to continually experiment with new ideas or else we can fall into a rut. We hope that by pushing ourselves, we will inspire you to push your boundaries, too. We ended up loving this look and think that it would be perfect for a modern autumn scheme, since it is both cool and warm. It can also be particularly practical for autumn, because many seasonal varieties of purple tones are available in the flower shops, from heather to dahlias, hydrangeas, impatiens, asters, coneflowers, and sweet peas.

In addition to our styling and arranging tips, we'll share sophisticated container ideas that work beautifully in a more grown-up scheme like this one. You will notice that our palette is quite classy and loaded with texture and sparkle with additions of metallic silver and gold, natural wood, crystal, reflective surfaces like mirror and stone, glass, and white porcelain. For our project idea, we'll share a fun DIY using wine bottles and glitter (we promise it's not cheesy!) and a sweet and very grown-up tea party that could easily make for the most lovely little Mother's Day brunch.

ELEGANT, REGAL, WARM, and **CLASSY,** neutral with a bit of pop can be just what the decorator ordered for a home that currently feels a bit drab by neutral overkill. Give it a try with a favorite accent color of your own and see what you can sprinkle in to create a little character.

101.

DECORATE
WITH
FLOWERS

In this elegant master bedroom designed by homeowner Mariana D'Amici we added a petite bedside bouquet of dark wine scabious, purple dahlias, and a sprig of orchids to a small mercury glass cup. In a neutral room, metallic and reflective finishes can make a potentially bland palette rich and dramatic. Touches of gold, silver, mirror, and sequins all work together to create an interesting, inviting room.

A gold glass cake stand is a pedestal for a deeply toned bouquet in a gold-patterned Moroccan tea cup. Tied with a silver ribbon, this little bouquet looks festive when combined with gold and glass pieces. For special occasions the flowers do not need to be elaborate or expensive. Just purchase flowers in the same hue and combine them in a metallic cup.

Sometimes a large room needs a large arrangement. An easy way to approach a large arrangement is to just group like flowers together to create a backdrop for a few focal flowers at the front. Nothing complicated! Here we have tall delphiniums and some agonis branches at the back, some long-stemmed burgundy alstroemeria in the middle, and then some purple dahlias and a large hydrangea bloom at the front. Easy!

Sometimes three small vases can be an easy way to dress up a little table. A single dahlia, a purple dendrobium branch, and a few dark purple scabious are held in small silver vases. In a neutral room with pale colors the touch of dark purple and magenta in the table and flowers looks very elegant.

SPREAD THE LOVE AROUND YOUR HOME.

When hosting a special celebration it can be especially pretty to display several arrangements in one room. Try varying the scale and proportion of each arrangement: Try a low, wide bouquet on a coffee table, a small posy on a side table, and a few tall blooms on a cabinet or shelf. Put extra time and effort into the one that your guests will be seated closest to. Then you can set aside a few flowers to create the posy, and a few long stems for the tall arrangement. For the coffee table, try using a low square glass vase. Vary the flower sizes—large round blooms can fill up space, like hydrangea, and then work with medium-sized flowers, like tulips, and a few spiky delphiniums and the fluffy texture of heather.

103.

MOODY MIX

Crisp white bone china from Germany, some vintage and others from the Rosenthal studio line, provides a striking, moody contrast against a dark gray bookcase when showcasing lush shades of garden rose, tulips, variegated hosta leaves, coxcomb, allium, and poppies.

FLORAL FOCUS

This large-scale arrangement becomes the grand focal point in a Vancouver living room. A French glazed pedestal vase, handmade in Paris by Astier de Villatte, is filled with purple hydrangea, burgundy alstroemeria, and eucalyptus leaves and seed pods.

ADD CONTRAST IN SMALL DOSES TO GIVE A MOSTLY NEUTRAL SPACE AN UNEXPECTED JOLT.

A PRETTY AND PROPER AFTERNOON TEA

Fancy a spot of tea? There is something special about taking tea in the afternoon, though few of us have time to do it! That's why you have to buy out time, put on your favorite dress, and spoil yourself and your dear friends. A ladies' afternoon tea time means pausing for a few hours to share special moments (and a little gossip!) and can even make for a most intimate Mother's Day celebration. This classy setting can't fail to effortlessly delight and impress.

Entertaining ideas

DAHLIAS ON DISPLAY

Tall, cylindrical glass vases display purple dahlias that sit just below the rim with a few flower heads afloat along the bottom. This display idea is a real stunner in a minimalistic modern home.

We've kept the look light and bright by mingling smooth white porcelain with polished crystal along with Earl Grey tea and sweets topped with non-toxic organic blooms. For a personal touch, we've added hand-tied posy arrangements (our how-to is on pages 18–19) that each guest can take away, consisting of tulips, dendrobium orchids, dahlias, scabious, and alstroemeria. Tip: With a little modification, this grown-up tea party can also suit a gathering of little girls.

THE POWER OF COLOR

This dining space is bathed in natural light in a pure white setting, with just the right amount of shine through the silver and gold metallics brought in through the Love Candy posters from Made By Girl, silver Moroccan pendant light, and silver hardware on the cabinetry. Adding touches of color through flowers, you can change up a neutral space in seconds. Our red and violet tones, all from the same color family, could easily be swapped with any color "families" that you love for a similar look.

DECORATE
WITH
FLOWERS

you will need:
wine bottles, flat white spray paint, metallic glitter, craft glue, a sponge brush, paper

1.

2.

3.

4.

method:

1. Rinse out the bottles and then remove all labels and residue. When dry, spray paint with a flat white spray paint. Using matte paint will give the bottles a more porcelain-looking finish, rather than a glossy paint finish. At least two coats of paint are necessary—make sure you allow the paint to dry between coats for a smoother look.

2. When dry apply a thin layer of craft glue to a small area of the bottle and then add glitter. Place a piece of paper under the bottle before you apply the glitter.

3. Work your way around the bottle. Making an organic wavy band is easier than attempting a straight line.

4. Fold the paper and pour excess glitter back into its container for re-use.

FLOWERS USED
    IN THIS PROJECT:
* Carnation
* Snapdragon
* Spray chrysanthemum
* 'James Storie' orchid

We simply had to include a section dedicated to all things **FEMININE, ZESTY,** and **FLIRTY THAT OOZE "LA" STYLE,** at least how we see it, particularly since we have such a strong connection to Southern California and our friends there. We also love to work with joyful palettes in our home, office, even our wardrobe, so this style clicks for us. And it's happy! Who doesn't love feeling happy?

This look embraces a broad mix of eclectic flea market finds coupled with vibrant and cheerful splashes of color, bold geometric prints, and gorgeous pottery. Bold, sunny colors combined with heaps of gold and warm wooden mid-century pieces are the hallmarks of this peppy style. It's definitely NOT for the minimalist—it's full-on with plenty of attention to detail, from the lighting down to the stacks of books artfully placed on shelves and coffee tables. We work with various tones of **BLUE AND VIOLET WITH A CITRUSY MIX OF ORANGE, RED,** and **YELLOW** and bright, sculptural flowers that range from lotus pod, delphinium, pink ranunculus, and red viburnum berries to bougainvillea and a variety of orchids. Girly glam is flirty without being too sweet and very bold—it's the best friend you'd love to have, a style guru, your ultimate girl crush.

This look is great if you're in a color rut or just feel a bit bleh about your décor. It's also terrific for renters; in fact the homes in this section all belong to renters and we think it's quite fab how they've given their spaces such a personal touch. If your home is lacking warmth and style, we always suggest looking to nature—flowers and plants—for an instant boost, along with simple and often affordable decorative accessories to provide the quickest and easiest ways for a little revamp. Throw pillows, scented candles, a grouping of sweet treasures on a tray atop a coffee table, artwork found at flea markets and on sites like Etsy and eBay, an inviting throw rug to sink your toes into . . . All of the little thoughtful touches add up to introduce color, texture, your personality, and a definite mood. We all wish to create a special atmosphere at home, don't you think?

We've packed this section with loads of decorating tips and we've pulled out the bubbly for our entertaining idea too—a swanky cocktail hour with the girls. You'll also find our unique and super quick DIY project incorporating stickers (yes, really!) and spray paint to make the most clever glass containers—we enjoy making things for our homes and hope you'll try all of our projects in this book, but if time permits, at least try this one. We guarantee you'll love it.

You cannot help but smile as you enter happy-go-lucky rooms like the ones we're about to share, so enjoy! As you flip through this section, think of ways you can bring a little sunshine into your home by examining these exciting LA interiors that belong to a few of our stylish friends.

FLIRTATIOUS, FIERY, VIBRANT, and **BOLD** Girly Glam isn't for the color shy!

113.

DECORATE
WITH
FLOWERS

WORKING THE ROOM FOR FULL-ON COLOR

The bold geometric pillow provided the inspiration for this living room arrangement (left). Various tones of bright pink, red, purple, and green work well together when they can be tied to something else in the room that has a similar palette. Sometimes artwork can provide inspiration for the palette of an arrangement you want to create. A deep blue ceramic vase works perfectly with the artwork next to it (below). Here, blue delphiniums, magenta zinnias, wine-colored astrantia, and white asclepias pick up colors used in the painting. The yellow oncidium gives the arrangement a bright lift and works well to tie in the color of the maplewood cabinet.

This side table arrangement is also inspired by the painting next to it. The bright bunch adds an even more colorful punch in this room when its palette is pulled directly from the nearby artwork.

We added some square gold confetti to this vase, which catches the light and adds a little glam to this arrangement. Gomphrena, nerine, and dahlias are gathered and placed in the glittering water.

A cup filled with orange dahlias and purple bougainvillea brightens up this bedside table and works well with the fluffy orange throw pillow (above).

A dark teal vase paired with green lotus pods and privet berries works nicely with the painting and seating in the dining area. Red anemones and dark pink ranunculus give a shot of color (right). A bottle label inspired us to bring in orange for the cocktail table bouquet (above).

SECRETS OF A STYLIST

We could easily curl up in this bold bedroom belonging to LA stylist Emily Henderson. Her whimsical touches and love of vintage pieces are reflected throughout her home and the bedroom is no exception. Notice how the deep blue velvet headboard is punctuated by the bold fuchsia pendant light and the striped throw at the foot of the bed. Most stylists work in odd numbers. With color accenting, it's no different. It helps to keep the eye moving around a space without any "holes" and simply looks better. In this case, the third pop of fuchsia was added through a small arrangement using clematis, dahlia, rose, astrantia, and waxflower on her nightstand, a small yet bold touch.

PUT A RING ON IT

We love the home of LA blogger
and graphic designer Bri Emery and
wanted to bring a special touch to her
bedroom by adding a playful floral
accent to suit her charming, spirited
personality. We quickly thought of
a floral wreath using her signature
colors, yellow and pink, to add a bit
of color to her headboard and play off
the arrangements on the table along
with her Moroccan rag rug.

HOW WE MADE IT:

Create a wire form out of heavy-gauge florist wire. Wrap the
wire with white floral tape. As with the project on pages 36–
37, wrap a small assortment of flowers together with floral
tape to create a posy. We used a dahlia, mint, waxflower, and
a yellow spray rose. Attach the wrapped posy stems to the
wire form with more floral tape. Do the whole process again
to create another small posy and then attach it. Add some
ribbon by starting with a dab of hot glue. Then wrap the
ribbon around the stem area and loosely around the wire
form. Leave some long pieces to trail down if you like.

TOUCHES OF COLOR IN A ROOM CAN BE HIGHLIGHTED WITH FLOWERS. A BOLD GRAPHIC ON THE SPINE OF A BOOK AND SOME TASSELS ON A PILLOW INSPIRED THIS BRIGHT ASSORTMENT ON THE COFFEE TABLE.

STRIKING A BALANCE

A turquoise glazed vase was used to hold a few red orchids (below). Instead of having the arrangement pop, like the one on the coffee table (opposite), we wanted to keep this one subdued so the vase and flowers worked as a complementary accessory on the shelves.

SIDE PROJECT

For this sleek table we used flowers in the pink, magenta, violet, and red tones from the painting to create a low small arrangement in a round glass vase. The clear container doesn't compete with the lamps or the wooden vase we used for a few orchid branches.

BOLDER CHOICE

Here we wanted to show how you could also have a bold arrangement work with the art behind it. The silvery eucalyptus, cream ranunculus, and the vase work with the art behind and the bright red dahlias and berries add a punch of color.

ADD FLOWERS TO BOOKCASES AND DISPLAY OBJECTS IN SIMILAR SHAPES OR COLORS, IN THIS CASE YELLOW AND GOLD, TO BRING BALANCE AND HARMONY TO SHELVING.

UNITY AND FORM

This large mantle-top arrangement shows how well different flower forms can work together. First you have the line flowers—sculptural spheres of yellow oncidium—to lend height. Next, sprays of deep purple clematis add volume and movement—bringing the eye towards the focal flowers, the circular magenta dahlias. The yellow craspedia is added as a filler near the rim of the vase, which picks up the yellow oncidium to bring balance to the arrangement.

The Vintage Home JUDITH WILSON

MODERN PAPER CRAFTS Van Sicklen

DECORATE *workshop*

AT HOME WITH white ATLANTA BARTLETT

The Surreal Calder

ART AT THE TURN OF THE MILLENNIUM TASCHEN

AT HOME IN

New Paris Interiors

domino THE BOOK of DECORATING

JONATHAN ADLER MY PRESCRIPTION FOR ANTI-DEPRESSIVE LIVING

COLOR CRAFT

Entertaining ideas

COCKTAIL HOUR WITH THE GIRLS

We vote for less planning and more parties in life, so why not create something sweet that requires little effort so you can spend more time with those you love? This easy Friday night soirée can be whipped up in a flash with a spread of cheese, fresh bread, fruit, bubbly, and flowers. We've worked with magenta anemone, yellow and magenta spray roses, purple waxflower, pink dahlias, yellow ranunculus, and fresh mint since they accent the gorgeous hues in the rugs beneath the table. A few magical ideas with an elegant touch include scattering candles among small bouquets in sparkling gold Moroccan tea glasses to complement a gold metal cage with a porcelain base in the center of the table, also flower-filled.

CLUSTERS OF COLOR

Grouping small bouquets by a single hue is a quick way to arrange flowers when you don't have time to think about creating the perfect color combos. These magenta anemones are gorgeous displayed just as they are and a bunch of mint on a nearby bar cart adds color while encouraging a little mojito making!

PLAY GROUP
A stunning gilded metal cage on top of a porcelain base by designer Alessandro Dubini is a sweet incarnation of a bell jar and is a playful way to group a dahlia, some spray roses, and a cup of mint.

QUICK FIX

It is easy to misplace your glass at a party. A creative touch is to tie a different fresh bud to stem glassware with a dainty ribbon. For a bit of sparkle, add a faux golden leaf or something else with a little pizzazz that you have tucked away in your craft drawer. Cocktails, anyone?

123.

step-by-step project

STICKERS & GOLD PAINT
ON GLASS

HELLO

you will need:

glass florist vases, stickers, washi tape, gold spray paint

method:

1. Wash the vases and allow to dry. Apply stickers or tape to create your desired design. We used washi tape to create stripes, star stickers randomly placed for a fun pattern and alphabet stickers for our "Hello" vase.

2. Cover the outside of the vases with gold spray paint. Follow the spray paint directions to get an even coat. You may need to apply two coats; just make sure you allow each one to dry.

3. Carefully peel off the stickers or tape. This decoration is not water safe on the outside, so be very careful when filling the vase with water and cleaning.

1.

FLOWERS USED
 IN THIS PROJECT:
* Dahlia
* Statice
* Chrysanthemum
* Mint

2.

3.

chapter **8.** # BLACK & WHITE

When working with black and white, we love it when we see fearless homeowners who layer in bold prints and patterns and aren't afraid to paint a wall or a piece of furniture black. Let's face it, some need a bit of respite from all of the color in the world and are perfectly content in a monochromatic scheme. One thing we've noticed when we see this look done right is that it's all about the details. That is why we are instantly drawn in—because we both go ga-ga for detail and knew we'd have fun exploring this graphic mix. The question is, how do you work flowers into this scheme if you aren't keen on color?

For black and white, we're going with very little color in our flowers, using only bits of yellow and purple since we've set our focus on **BRINGING THE OUTDOORS IN THROUGH LUSH FOLIAGE IN WHITES AND GREENS**. To us, this is the perfect path for those who aren't keen on color but still wish to incorporate flowers.

In this section, we're presenting a more graphic, organic black and white style influenced by Scandinavian design. Monochromatic looks can vary; many are super contemporary and minimalistic, but the Scandi-inspired decorating style we're highlighting is our flavor of the moment. We love how warm woods are incorporated to create a cozy atmosphere and that **LAYERING GRAPHIC PATTERNS THROUGH ACCESSORIES, TEXTILES, AND ARTWORK IS EMBRACED**. It's less about glamour and perfection and more about taking a natural approach that we find unintimidating and very welcoming—not words you commonly associate with a black and white scheme, are they?

In this section, we'll share spaces in three different parts of the world to show you how style gurus all over are working within this limited palette. For the lovebirds out there, we've created a romantic anniversary dinner that you can try to recreate in your own way, or even scale down for a dinner for two. Our DIY project is versatile and fun, requires few supplies, and can be done in a flash—we invite you to get creative and take it as far as you want to go.

LAYERED, NATURAL, SCANDINAVIAN, GRAPHIC, EASY, and **AT-HOME,** this is one of the coziest takes on black and white we've seen. We hope you'll explore it for yourself whether on a moodboard, for a dinner party, or a little redecorating project. Be brave and have fun!

OXOXO

8

36

129.

DECORATE
WITH
FLOWERS

BRING NATURAL BEAUTY AND
TEXTURE TO SHELVING WITH
A PETITE CLUSTER OF DAHLIAS,
SCABIOUS, AND MINT.

HANG IT UP

For special occasions you can quickly pull together a flower garland using a strip of torn fabric, ribbons, and petite buds to display around a doorway, mirror, or to lay in strips down the center of a table. Tip: Use real flowers for a one-day event, faux if you need them to last longer.

TIGHTLY EDITED

Though flowers wilt and die quickly beneath glass, we still love how they look sitting beneath a cloche and find this edited display quite nice to pull together when expecting guests for only a few hours. Try bringing in a little baby's breath, a flower that is often referred to as grandmotherly, in your next arrangement—it is pretty when used as a base to display more graphic blooms.

MONOCHROME MEDLEY

A timeless combination of black and white can easily be created through a coat of paint and some imagination. The doors on this vintage Jugendstil cabinet were given a chalkboard treatment with a few coats of paint, and a desk drawer was repurposed and used as a moodboard to display black and white photography. Flowers in bell jars and a tall arrangement add height and a pop of fresh green to complete this corner.

BABY BLOOM

A spiky white dahlia in a bud vase and a small grouping of white tulips give this monochromatic nursery in Vancouver a touch of nature, while also serving to break up the strong contrasts with a bit of fresh green. Flowers in a nursery are a sweet touch, but only if you take a few precautions. First, it's best to use those that are fragrance-free since the scented variety can cause a loss of appetite and may inhibit your baby's sense of smell. Also be sure flowers are pollen-free, just in case your little one is sensitive. Keep flowers fresh by changing the water daily and when they begin to wilt it's time to toss them out. Finally, less is more. A single stem or tiny cluster is all that you need!

FIRST STOP EAT
BATH TIME
PYJAMAS
BRUSH TEETH
STORYTIME
PRAYERS
TUCK
KISS AND CUDDLE
SLEEPTIME

WHEN IT COMES TO FLOWERS IN **GRAPHIC SPACES**,
WE LOVE ARCHITECTURAL **BLOOMS** IN **TALL VASES**
TO **COMPLETE** THE SPACE.

FLOWER EXPLOSION

Most lovers of black and white don't particularly care for fussy, romantic arrangements near their desk. The pom-pom tops of purple allium, resembling fireworks frozen in mid-explosion, fit perfectly in this workspace—they add texture and life that is totally fuss-free.

AN **ORGANIC BURST OF BLOOMS**
IN THIS GRAPHIC, MODERN COTTAGE
CREATES A LITTLE MONOCHROME MAGIC.

POWER OF ONE

There are so many black and white décor options available these days that it only takes a visit to your local design store or a few keystrokes to find just the right piece. Graphic designer Tara Hurst fell in love fast with this cascading flowers print by Debbie Carlos and added it above a vintage wooden table in her dining room for a bold decorative element. To not detract from its beauty, a simple bundle of white buddleia was added as a soft touch, to introduce both dimension and texture.

SCENTS AND SENSIBILITY

When decorating your kitchen with flowers, opt for herbs to display and eat, or use flowers that aren't too fragrant to avoid sensory overload when preparing meals. Gerbera daisies are a favorite since you can find them anywhere and they create a cheery, uplifting atmosphere. Other fragrance-free types we recommend include sunflowers, tulips, Queen Anne's lace, dahlias, ranunculus, geraniums, anemones, carnations, most orchids, lisianthus, and hydrangea.

OUTSIDE IN

The living room corner in the San Francisco home of our dear friend and blogger Victoria Smith is given a visual lift with a black ceramic jug overflowing with white iris, variegated euphorbia, and white gomphrena. Don't be shy—bring in plants and flowers—after all, foliage is best friends with black and white!

Entertaining ideas

KISSES & HUGS
ANNIVERSARY DINNER

Every decorating idea begins with something that inspired it. For this anniversary dinner, porcelain cups designed by Arne Jacobsen became our jumping-off point. We selected four—two with Xs and two with Os, symbols for kisses and hugs to express love and good friendship—and added elegant calla lilies and purple privet berries, which sit atop black metal trays sprinkled with sequins and tea lights wrapped in graphic dotty washi tape. Table linens and dinnerware from House Doctor were added in a black and white scheme, cutlery is tied with black ribbon, and napkins are adorned with silver ribbon and an X taped on top. Place cards were made using rubber stamps on small folded cardstock, and a swirling plate of silver ribbons adds a shimmery finishing touch.

GO BEHIND THE SCENES

To maintain continuity in a space when decorating, you only have to add small touches of black and white to tie it all together. The lampshade was originally white but when shiny black tape and a flower brooch was added, it took on a new look. To reflect the candlelight and create a romantic atmosphere after sunset, a leaning mirror from the bedroom was added. Taping favorite photography found in magazines to the wall brought in more black and white with no expense. Black candles replace the typical white variety and privet berry sprigs were tied to the stems for a more festive touch. There's nothing wrong with moving things around to make your party more attractive, so think beyond the tabletop—you'll be surprised with what you can achieve!

Step-by-step project
GRAPHIC STAMPED BAGS

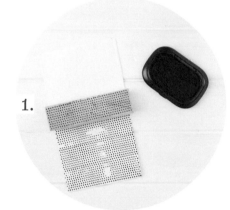

1.

2.

3.

method:

1. Create an all-over pattern on the bags using different stamps or just create a strong visual with one stamp.

2. Use pens and paint to make simple graphic freehand patterns on both sides of the bag.

3. Once the ink or paint is completely dry, open up your bag and place a jam jar inside to hold water for your flowers. If you like, you can trim the bag so that it is just higher than the jar—your flowers will then peep over the top.

**FLOWERS USED
   IN THIS PROJECT:**

✳ Alstroemeria

✳ Spray chrysanthemum

✳ Chrysanthemum

FLOWER FAVORITES

HERE ARE SOME OF OUR FAVORITE FLOWERS WITH TIPS ON HOW WE LOVE TO USE THEM AT HOME

ACHILLEA, or yarrow, can provide a dense texture to arrangements. We love the yellow and the white varieties as fillers. We also take apart white yarrow and use the tiny flowers as floating displays.

ALLIUM have round spheres of purple-hued flowers and they make a wonderful cut flower. We like to group them on their own in a tall vase; this way you can enjoy the beauty of their perfect round shape.

ALSTROEMERIA is often overlooked since it is so widely available. However, a large bouquet of white alstroemeria in a tall clear vase can look stunning, is affordable, and does not have a scent, which can be good when entertaining. The dark wine-colored variety gives drama to a bouquet.

ANEMONES are commonly found in intense jewel tones and have a black center. This combination makes them very dramatic looking. Place a bouquet in a mercury glass vase and you have a stunning combination for a party.

ASTERS, also referred to as Michaelmas daisies, are a common cut flower that can add that little bit of color you may be looking for. We especially like the pale purple, bright pink, and the white.

ASTILBES provide such pretty fluffy texture. We like the cream and soft pink varieties for our country-looking bouquets.

ASTRANTIA are not that common in flower shops, but can easily be ordered. They make a lovely cut flower as they stand quite straight and come in a silvery white and a light burgundy.

CHRYSANTHEMUMS, or just "Mums," are another one of those commonly found flowers at the supermarket or florist shop. We love to use the white 'China Mum' in bouquets because of their large bloom size and all the white petals.

DAHLIAS come in many sizes, from very large like the 'Café Peach' dahlias used in our Coastal chapter to the small ball-shaped ones like 'CG Spirit' in the Happy Brights chapter. Dahlias look great in a nice big bunch or they also work well on their own.

DELPHINIUMS have tall stems with many dark blue flowers. They also come in light blue and white. Their tall slim shape makes them a great addition to a bouquet to provide height and texture. We like using them with round-shaped flowers like dahlias.

GARDEN ROSES both 'Old' and 'Modern,' like the English David Austen roses, are wonderful in bouquets when in season. Their gorgeous fragrance and plethora of petals make them a favorite for special occasions and celebrations. Stunning on their own or paired with other flowers, they have the "wow" factor that is hard to match.

HYDRANGEA's large flower heads make them easy to use in your home, as they look stunning in a simple bunch of about five stems in a large milk jug. Their gorgeous blue is hard to replicate with anything else. We also love using the white variety for its pillow-like mound of flowers.

LAVENDER looks lovely freshly picked and added to an arrangement for a "garden" look. It also has a long history of culinary and medical uses, making it appropriate for a kitchen bouquet or a posy near the bathtub.

LYSIMACHIA, also called gooseneck, is a flower that we enjoy because of the tapering spike shape of white blossoms. It can provide that much-needed interesting shape when you have mainly round flowers.

NERINE add an exotic look to arrangements. We often use the pale pink and the white varieties. However, they do come in more intense shades as well. They make an excellent cut flower and last quite well. The flowers look especially elegant off the stem floating in a pretty shallow bowl.

ORCHIDS can add an interesting exotic look. They are excellent cut flowers and last a long time. We used purple, white, and rusty red dendrobiums and yellow oncidiums in this book. They look elegant as a single stem or add an unexpected punch of color in a larger arrangement.

PEONIES are similar to Old Garden roses when it comes to the "wow" factor. Maybe it is all those petals, or their subtle fragrance. During peony season there are many varieties available.

POPPIES come in gorgeous shades. The opium poppy is a delicate and exceptionally beautiful cut flower. We love the quirky stems and buds. Occasionally we splurge on Icelandic poppies—their crinkled paper-like petals are irresistible.

QUEEN ANNE'S LACE has a flat umbrella of white flowers and grows like a weed. A large bunch is really pretty in a tall cylinder vase. They have a delicate airy look that is stunning for a daytime event.

RANUNCULUS, with their pretty ruffled petals, come in a wide variety of colors, from intense jewel tones to soft pinks and white. They have a smaller flower head than peonies and roses, making them easy to incorporate into any bouquet. They have no scent, making them perfect to run along a dining table in pretty cups.

SCABIOUS, more commonly know as the pincushion flower, works very well as a cut flower. Their slightly curving stems creates a unique element in a bouquet. They commonly come in a lovely creamy white, a pale blue, a pale purple, and a dramatic dark wine that can look almost black.

SEDUMS are succulents, with a waxy texture to their stems and foliage. They are an interesting cut flower because of their tiny florets that grow in clusters to create pretty mounds of color. The sedums we use commonly come in green and pinks; we mainly used 'Autumn Joy.'

SOLIDAGO, or goldenrod, are similar looking to astilbe, but we use them for their distinct bright yellow color. They are an easy-to-use filler, with straight stems. We love pairing them with white flowers and greens.

TULIPS are another common flower we love to use in our homes because of their wide availability and all the fabulous colors they come in. Some favorite varieties are the two-toned parrot tulips, the pale peach, the bright yellow, the two-toned pale pink and white, and the dark purple tulip.

WE LOVE THESE
EDIBLE BLOOMS:
✳ Note ✳
Choose only
organic, and use
only the flower
or petals;
remove stems,
pistils, and
stamen.

Apple blossom
Calendula
Carnation
Chamomile
Chive blossom
Chrysanthemum
Dandelion
English daisy
Geranium (scented)
Lavender
Lemon Blooms
Lilac
Marigold
Nasturtium
Orchid
Pansy
Rose
Sunflower
Viola

DECORATE
WITH
FLOWERS

OUR LITTLE BLACK BOOK

HERE ARE A FEW OF OUR RESOURCES FOR PRETTY THINGS WE'VE USED THROUGHOUT THIS BOOK. WE LIST MANY MORE AT DECORATEWITHFLOWERS.COM, INCLUDING FAVORITE FLORISTS AND OUR MANY BLOGGER FRIENDS WHO INSPIRE US, SO PLEASE VISIT US THERE!

UNITED STATES

FLORAL AND CRAFT SUPPLIES

32° North
Specialty craft supplies including European paper scraps, fabric millinery flowers, and gorgeous trims.
vintage-ornaments.com

Bell'occhio
We shopped here together while in San Francisco and emerged totally inspired but with an empty wallet—the ribbons alone will make you drool!
bellocchio.com

Caramelos
We are huge fans of everything in this shop because it is lovingly curated and filled with uncommon finds like tiny German mushrooms (sweet to add to your bouquets or boutonnieres).
etsy.com/shop/caramelos

Create for Less
Online mega store with discounted craft supplies.
createforless.com

Cute Tape
Baker's twine and string like that shown on page 96, cute bags similar to our chevron bags on page 78, and loads of washi tape for taping onto your glass vases to add a special touch.
cutetape.com

Flax Art + Design
A wonderful store for gathering ribbon, twine, paper, and stamps.
flaxart.com

The Gilded Bee
A fantastic online haberdashery and paper shop.
etsy.com/shop/thegildedbee

Impress
Excellent selection of rubber stamps similar to those shown on pages 138–39.
impressrubberstamps.com

Jamali Garden
Silk flowers for mixing into real bouquets or for taping on the wall or onto garlands, and oodles of floral supplies.
jamaligarden.com

Michaels
Large selection of glues, spray paint, and containers such as bottles (shown on pages 60, 61, and 93) and a variety of glass vases.
michaels.com

Martha Stewart Crafts
We love her paper punches, paper goods, paint, and glitter (like those shown on pages 50 and 108).
marthastewartcrafts.com

Olive Manna
Twine in unique colors, mini clothespins, and tags in all sizes, similar to those shown on page 35, lovely labels, bags, and vintage bell jars.
etsy.com/shop/OliveManna

Oriental Trading
An online shop jam-packed with craft and hobby supplies with a focus on bulk ordering.
orientaltrading.com

Paper Source
This shop always sparks new, creative ideas whenever we visit. Their papers from around the world and craft bags are always faves.
paper-source.com

Purl Soho
A fabric lover's dream and a great resource for Liberty London textiles (shop online!) in the USA, as shown on pages 64 and 66–67.
purlsoho.com

Save on Crafts
Lovely selection of twinkle lights that add such a special ambiance when decorating, as seen on pages 35 and 49.
save-on-crafts.com

Shop Sweet Lulu
Great source for mason jars shown throughout this book along with the milk bottles on page 79 that are inside the chevron bags, and those featured on page 89.
shopsweetlulu.com

Studio Carta
Beyond fabulous trims and twines.
angelaliguori.com

Tinsel Trading
Amazing vintage flowers (perfect for mixing into real arrangements) and gorgeous trim.
tinseltrading.com

CONTAINERS AND TABLEWARE

Anthropologie
Inspiring to visit for their displays alone but also fun to shop for vases and containers that you could easily use for flowers, along with loads of other things. This is a must-shop!
anthropologie.com

Jonathan Adler
This is one of our favorite designers—we love the quirky vases in his signature mid-century style, especially those with faces!
jonathanadler.com

Koromiko
Inspiring handmade vessels and planters that are both well made and rare.
koromiko.com

Leif
A colorful haven for planters and vases. Side note: They also have some fabulous botanical prints printed with vibrant inks that we adore to display in the home!
leifshop.com

Pottery Barn
Everything for the tabletop, including vases and other vessels that you could easily repurpose for flowers.
potterybarn.com

Terrain
A little something for gardeners and flower lovers everywhere. They also stock flowerpots, like those used on page 66, quality floral pruners and shears, along with beautiful containers for flowers.
shopterrain.com

West Elm
Great source for all that you need to lay the perfect table. They also stock cloches similar to those shown on pages 88 and 131.
westelm.com

CANADA

CONTAINERS AND TABLEWARE

Chintz and Company
Carries a wide variety of glass vases in all sizes as well as an extensive tabletop selection. The Victoria store is a favorite.
chintz.com

The Cross
A stunning home décor store with a wide selection of vases and tableware for arrangements of any size. The Cross generously loaned us some lovely props seen in this book.
thecrossdesign.com

FLORAL AND CRAFT SUPPLIES

Masterstroke Canada
Absolute ribbon heaven!
masterstrokecanada.com

Michaels
A great place to find just about anything, including the hoops shown on the wall on page 93 (just insert pieces of fabric and hang!).
michaels.com

Opus Art Supply
A great selection of spray paints to re-purpose your containers.
opusartsupplies.com

Spool of Thread
A wonderful fabric store in Vancouver that carries excellent prints for some of the projects in this book.
spoolofthread.com

Uguisu
A Japanese online shop that ships globally, a go-to for washi tape and papers to dress up your containers.
uguisustore.com

WITH THANKS

PHOTOGRAPHY

Photos by **Leslie Shewring** unless noted below.

Laure Joliet Pages: 16, 86, 87, 88, 90 (top), 91, 94, 95, 110 (left, right), 111 (left, right), 114, 115, 116, 117, 118, 119, 120, 121, 122, 123, 126 (center), 130, 134, 135 (center right, bottom left). laurejoliet.com

Janis Nicolay Pages: 3, 6 (right), 43, 48, 49, 53 (center), 58, 59, 62, 63, 64, 65, 68 (left, right), 69 (left, right), 72, 73, 74, 75, 76, 77, 78, 79, 98 (left, right), 99 (center, right), 102, 103, 105, 106, 107, 132, 143 (left). janisnicolay.com

Thorsten Becker Pages: 6 (left), 131 (top, bottom), 136, 137, 143 (right).alternatewords.com

Holly Becker Pages: 47 (center), 111 (center), 131 (center). decor8blog.com

MODELS

Bri Emery, pages 122, 123 designlovefest.com

Jessica Senti, page 64 jessicasenti.com

Caitlin Sheehan, pages 2, 141 admiralandtea.typepad.com,

Sienna Sheehan, page 53 (right)

LOCATIONS

Along with our studio spaces in Victoria, British Columbia, and Hannover, Germany, we've included many views from these lovely homes in North America. A special thank you to each homeowner for generously welcoming us into your homes to photograph for this book—we are so thankful!

Rachel Ashwell rachelashwellshabbychiccouture.com

Kate Campbell kateandcampbell.com

Donato & Mariana D'Amici damicidesign.com

Bri Emery

designlovefest.com

Joanna Fletcher

Emily Henderson stylebyemilyhenderson.com

Tara Hurst tarahurst.com

Kate Horsman bulletwithbutterflywings.ca

Nancy Riesco riescolapres.com

Victoria Smith sfgirlbybay.com

PROPS

We'd like to thank Megan Close at The Cross, Tina Pedersen from Agentur Pedersen, House Doctor, and Charlotte Hedeman Guéniau at Rice for lending us the many props used throughout this publication.

The Cross thecrossdesign.com

Agentur Pedersen agenturpedersen.com

House Doctor housedoctor.dk

Rice rice.dk

ARTISTS

Pages 55, 64, 65 Zoe Pawlak; page 72 Rifle Paper Co; page 71 Perry Kavitz, pages 71, 72 Donna Wilson; page 74 top left Leanda Xavian, top center Step Back, top right Elizabeth Bauman, center L. Minato, bottom right Third Drawer Down, below center Perry Kavitz; page 75 Perry Kavitz; page 77 Leah MacFarlane; page 79 top A. Stubbs; pages 85, 88 Hilda Grahnat, Allison Long Hardy; page 95 Jake Ashwell; pages 101, 107 Jennifer Ramos; pages 113, 114 Penine Hart; page 115 Joyce Lee; pages 118, 119 Michelle Armas; page 121 Danielle Krysa, Happy Red Fish; pages 122, 123 Max Wanger; pages 126, 129, 130 Lisa Congdon; pages 129, 130 top left, center, and bottom right Rikkianne Van Kirk; page 132 top center Mariana D'Amici, bottom left World of Maps, bottom right Kardz Couture; page 135 Debbie Ramos

WITH THANKS FROM HOLLY

While working on this book, I was also expecting my first child, so I channeled much of the energy and joy from my pregnancy into these pages—so a big thank you to my darling baby, my muse, who is due to arrive only a few months before publication. Your daddy and I cannot wait to share our life with you! A big kiss to my sweet husband **Thorsten** for all of your love and support; you are my rock and I am so grateful that you encouraged me to take my writing seriously because I cannot imagine my life without books or my blog! To my dear friends and fans of decor8—thank you for your support, I couldn't follow my career dreams without you. **Helen Bratby**—I am so grateful for the innumerable hours that you so generously gave us to design this book, along with your endless patience, creativity, and support. Thank you dear **Sian Parkhouse** for editing our book and making our vision a reality. Thank you **Jacqui Small and team**, and **Laura Lee Mattingly and Chronicle Books**, for giving us the opportunity to produce something from our hearts and for believing in this project. Thank you **Rebecca Friedman** for your support on my journey. A massive thanks to my assistant, **Jessy Senti**, you're the best! To **Laure Joliet** and **Janis Nicolay**—thank you for your beautiful photographs. A big thanks to our homeowners for letting us add lots of flower power to your home for the day. To my rock-star friend **Leslie Shewring**, thank you so much for everything! I cherish you immensely and love how beautiful my life and our book is because you're part of it. xo

WITH THANKS FROM LESLIE

This is my first book and I realized quite quickly the amount of help needed to get it all done. Firstly, thank you **Mom**. Thank you for blazing that creative artist mother trail for me to walk along so easily. Your love, generosity, and support inspire me daily. Thank you **Holly Becker** for wanting the best for me and for pulling me along. You see what I am capable of way before I even get a glimpse. Thank you **Jacqui Small** for this opportunity. You have a wonderful team who are a pleasure to work with. Especially **Sian Parkhouse**, our editor—thank you for your guidance. Thank you **Helen Bratby** for your brilliant design and supportive way. I hope to work with you again. Thank you **Laure Joliet** and **Janis Nicolay** for your stunning work. It was an absolute pleasure working with both of you and I feel very lucky to have had the opportunity. Thank you **Jessy Senti**—you are a special lady and your assistance in Vancouver was invaluable. Thank you **Caitlin** for always being up for anything—modeling for the book and babysitting at a moment's notice! Thank you **Diane** for being such a good sport, and sister. I am incredibly grateful for your willingness to lend a helping hand time and time again during this project. Thank you **Sienna** and **Parker** for being so understanding of your busy mother. And, of course, thank you **Dan**—you help make everything possible and way better.